Washington walked here

George
Washington's
250th
BIRTHDAY
COMMEMORATIVE
EDITION
NSDAR

**Published by
The National Society
Daughters of the American Revolution**

Washington walked here

Alexandria on the Potomac

Midway between Mount Vernon and The White House

by Mollie Somerville

Original edition published in 1970 by
Acropolis Books Ltd., Colortone Build-
ing, 2400 17th Street, N.W., Washington,
D.C. 20009

Printed in the United States of America by
Colortone Press, Creative Graphics Inc.,
Washington, D.C. 20009

Library of Congress Catalogue Number
70-109346
Standard Book No. 87491-126-5

Unless otherwise noted, all references to
Alexandria are to Alexandria, Virginia.

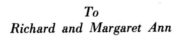

To
Richard and Margaret Ann

Acknowledgments

I am indebted most of all to Miss Ellen Coolidge Burke, Director of the Alexandria Library, who supported this undertaking when I began work on the book and encouraged me when I despaired of completing it. Her competent staff assisted me in the research along the way. I thank them all and also these librarians: College of William & Mary, Mr. James A. Servies; Enoch Pratt Free Library, Miss Elizabeth C. Litsinger; The Public Library of Washington, D.C., Miss Edith Ray Saul and Miss Georgia Cowan; the Virginia State Library, Mr. Milton C. Russell.

I thank the following organizations and their members who helped me in special areas: Mount Vernon Estate, Mr. Charles Cecil Wall, Miss Christine Meadows, Mr. Frank Morse, Mr. John A. Castellani; Historic Alexandria Foundation, Mrs. Hugh B. Cox; Alexandria City Hall, Mrs. Elizabeth McIver, Mrs. Patsy Altizer, Miss Katherine Bradfield, Mr. Eugene L. Barnwell, Mr. Don Heinemann, Mr. Ward L. Rothgeb; Alexandria Board of Trade, Mrs. Goldie Murphy; Fairfax County Courthouse, Mr. Thomas P. Chapman, Jr.; Gunston Hall, Mr. Frederick J. Griffiths, Mrs. Stalma Neill; Woodlawn Plantation, Mr. Meredith Johnson; Fort Belvoir, Mr. Edward B. Russell; Smithsonian Institution, Mr. C.

Malcolm Watkins; George Washington Masonic National Memorial, Mr. Edward Buckmaster; Southern Railway System, Mr. B. E. Young; Stable-Leadbeater Apothecary Shop, Mr. Robert D. Pearson; Carlyle House, Mr. L. D. Schaeffer; Daughters of the American Revolution, Mount Vernon Chapter.

I especially thank those who read and criticized the manuscript: Miss Ellen Coolidge Burke, Mr. Charles Cecil Wall, Mr. Frank Morse, Mr. Frederick J. Griffiths, Miss Cornelia B. Rose, Jr., Mr. and Mrs. Robert G. Whitton.

A number of people helped me with the illustrations in the book. I thank Mr. William Francis Smith, Mrs. John Howard Joynt, Mr. Norman Hatch, Miss Virginia Daiker of the Prints & Photographs Division of the Library of Congress, Mrs. Katharine M. Smith of the Virginia State Library, and Mr. and Mrs. Howard B. Marler for all they did.

Scores of Alexandrians invited me to their homes and let me look at old family letters, diaries, and memorabilia. Others shared their knowedge or recollections with me. I thank all those who extended such courtesies to me. Among them were: Mr. Worth Bailey, State Senator Leroy S. Bendheim, Mr. Marshall J. Beverley, Mrs. Ella Shannon Bowles, Mr. S. Cooper Dawson, Jr., Mrs. Lawrence Fawcett, Miss Esther Green, Mrs. Bruce C. Gunnell, Governor and Mrs. Richard B. Lowe, Mrs. Herbert E. Marshburn, Mrs. Charles Beatty Moore, Mr. Robert New, Mr. Delos Smith, Mrs. James M. Sprouse, and Captain and Mrs. E. K. Van Swearingen.

Lastly, I thank my family and friends for their sympathetic patience at those times when I was discouraged. Their affectionate understanding gave me the moral support to continue to the end.

Mollie Somerville

Contents

*"Prosperity to the town and the
citizens of Alexandria."*

Toast by George Washington
March 25, 1797

George Washington as a Young Surveyor by John Gadsby Chapman.

CHAPTER ONE

Prelude

Although George Washington left no lineal descendants, he was associated with so much of Alexandria's beginnings that he still seems a part of it. Alexandria is in a true sense his heir. As a gangling youth of seventeen, he helped survey the town in 1749. Later, Washington the soldier drilled his troops in the Market Square. The list continues: he worshipped at Christ Church, was appointed a town trustee, was master of the Masonic Lodge, endowed the town's free school, voted there, patronized its first bank, bought medicines at the local Apothecary Shop, danced at the assemblies in Gadsby's Tavern, attended plays and transacted business in Alexandria. And sometimes, when it was too late to go back to Mount Vernon, he spent the night in his own house built for such a purpose.

13

George Washington's Townhouse in Alexandria, a reconstruction. Washington had so much business in Alexandria that it was often too late in the evening to return to Mount Vernon. He spent many nights in the house he built in Alexandria.

Alexandria is situated on the Potomac River, in Virginia, between Mount Vernon and Washington, D.C. Today it is a prosperous city of 118,000 residents. Many are employed by the Federal government at Fort Belvoir and the Pentagon in Virginia, and in Washington, but large numbers work for a variety of industries, electronics in particular. These people live in the old town because they prefer it to new suburbia or cosmopolitan Washington. Historic Alexandria, George Washington's hometown, appeals greatly to newcomers. But many of today's Alexandria residents had forefathers among the town's founders. It is this combination of the new and old that gives the quaint old seaport town its unique character.

Alexandria originated from the custom in early Virginia of encouraging trade by attempting to establish towns along the rivers. Many of these so-called paper towns never advanced beyond the planning stage and exist only in the pages of musty old records. A few did flourish for a short time, but then disappeared. Of the thirty-one towns created in Virginia to promote trade, no other one has attained the size and importance of Alexandria, created in 1748.

The legislative act listed the names of the twelve trustees appointed to govern Alexandria. Heading the

Richard Barrett Lowe, Alexandria

Replica of George Washington's Townhouse on the original site at 508 Cameron St. The house was built by Washington in 1769 and torn down in 1855. The present restoration was erected in 1960.

15

Bessie Wilmarth Gahn

George Washington's Townhouse in Alexandria, from a sketch by Mary Stuart. The present house is a replica on the original site of the house built by Washington in 1769. The house was torn down in 1855.

list was Thomas, sixth Lord Fairfax. It was His Lordship's first post in America, and the beginning of Alexandria's connection with the titled family, a link that lasted for three generations, with Virginia's only long-term resident English nobility maintaining homes in and near Alexandria. Lord Fairfax's hunting lodge, Greenway Court, was about sixty-five miles inland, on the frontier of the New World where George Washington, as an apprentice surveyor, had helped survey the Fairfax land. The lodge was built on part of the five million acres that Lord Fairfax owned in the colony, and he lived at Greenway Court until his death.

After the death of the seventh Lord Fairfax, who lived in England, two Alexandrians succeeded to the title. Bryan, the eighth Lord Fairfax, was the son of Colonel Fairfax of Belvoir. Before the title descended to

16

The Fairfax family were Virginia's only long-term resident nobility maintaining homes in and near Alexandria. Lord Thomas Fairfax's hunting lodge, Greenway Court, was about sixty-five miles inland, near the present-day city of Winchester, Va. As an apprentice surveyor, George Washington helped survey the Fairfax land there.

him, he had been ordained and served as rector at Christ Church in Alexandria, and also at the Falls Church in adjoining Fairfax County. He was a lifelong friend of Washington's, and General and Mrs. Washington were godparents to one of his children. Washington's last meal away from home was at the eighth Lord Fairfax's estate, Mount Eagle, on the outskirts of Alexandria.

The ninth Lord Fairfax was Bryan Fairfax's eldest son, Thomas, who inherited the title in 1802.* His beautiful and architecturally distinctive residence on Cameron Street is still one of the loveliest buildings in the old town.

* The current, and fourteenth, Lord Fairfax is Nicholas John Albert, born 1956. (Burke's Genealogical and Heraldic History of the Landed Gentry—London, 1967.)

17

Belvoir, home of Colonel William Fairfax, Fairfax County, Virginia. After the Fairfax family returned to England in 1773, the mansion and its contents were put up for sale. George Washington was one of the purchasers and among the items he bought was a cast iron fireback from one of the many fireplaces. The fireback, a lining formerly placed in the back of fireplaces, is now in the Fort Belvoir Museum.

CHAPTER TWO

The Tobacco Economy

These members of the Fairfax family, unlike many of their plantation and town friends, were not primarily dependent on Virginia's single money crop, tobacco. But tobacco was an important factor in the early history of Alexandria, and dominated life in colonial Virginia. Tobacco, or the tobacco note, forerunner of a bank check, paid taxes, debts and salaries, bought imported goods as well as more land to produce more tobacco to pay more taxes and buy more luxuries. A tobacco planter's wealth depended upon the number, quality, and price of the hogsheads of tobacco he exported. The money due him was credited to his account by the firm overseas to which it was consigned and the account was drawn against in future transactions.

One day Sir Walter Raleigh boasted to Queen Elizabeth I that he could weigh tobacco smoke. The Queen wagered that he could not. Raleigh weighed a

Tobacco dominated the life of early Virginia. It was so important that it was used in place of money, and tobacco notes such as the one pictured above were accepted as legal tender.

small amount of tobacco, filled his pipe with it, smoked it, and then weighed the ash that was left. The difference in the two weights, he concluded, could only be accounted for by the smoke. Laughing, the Queen paid the amount of the bet and said: "Many alchemists have I heard of who turned gold into smoke, but where is one other who has turned smoke into gold?"

In the early eighteenth century, when Virginia was still sparsely settled, the colony's many rivers provided sufficient landing wharves alongside the tobacco fields so that ships could stop at each planter's wharf to take his tobacco on board. First, the manufactured products that the planter had ordered were unloaded. The bulk of these imports were household furnishings and clothing: a silk dress fabric for the planter's wife (the matching thread for making it up carefully included in the order), a pair of riding boots for the planter. George Washington's orders ranged from silver shoe buckles for Mrs. Washington's children to a family chariot.

However, this pick-up-and-delivery system had its drawbacks even when riverfront land was plentiful. The captain and his crew often had to wait offshore for the tobacco casks to be brought to the landing. Delays in loading could be serious: winter might set in before all the stops along the many rivers were made. And a frozen waterway could be financially ruinous to those planters on the captain's list whom his ship had not been able to reach.

As riverfront land became scarce and tobacco had to be transported from the back country by mules and horses instead of just rolled onto the waiting ships by sailors, this system failed to meet the needs of the planters in the interior. At about the same time, new colonial government regulations required that public warehouses be built for storing, weighing and inspecting the tobacco awaiting shipment. It was for this reason that by 1732 there was a warehouse on the northernmost boundary of the future site of Alexandria, at the foot of what is now Oronoco Street.

These tobacco warehouses were sometimes called rolling houses, and the roads that lead to them were known as rolling roads. Both names trace their origin to the way in which the enormous hogsheads of tobacco, which averaged about a thousand pounds, were brought to the rivers. Spikes were fixed to the ends or a rod was run through the center of these over-sized barrels. Saplings were attached to form shafts and power was furnished by a horse, an ox, or a mule. Thus the tobacco cask, serving as both container and conveyor, was rolled to its destination.

It is an appropriate coincidence that the name Potomac, an Algonquian word, means "a trading place." Even before the warehouse was built at the Alexandria site, there was a boat landing on this spot. Ferries were usually the only certain means for crossing rivers at that time. Bridges built in the upper, and narrower, regions of the rivers were continually being washed away by floods. The one main road linking the widely spaced

21

A colonial Virginia planter's wealth depended upon the quantity, price, and quality of the hogheads of tobacco he exported. These hogheads were rolled on board ship from each town's tobacco warehouse or planter's wharf.

towns along the Atlantic seaboard from north to south crossed the Potomac River at this point, and a ferry shuttled on call between Virginia and Maryland. In Virginia, this section of the road was originally an Indian trail that the planters first called the Potomac Path and later the King's Highway. This famous old road still passes through Alexandria as U.S. Highway No. 1.

Tobacco was such an important source of income to the mother country that England used every possible method to increase the amount of the crop grown in Virginia. Enormous quantities of tobacco were laden at Alexandria wharves and shipped to British merchants during the town's earliest days. But when tobacco crops grew less and less profitable to the planters near Alexandria, they grew more wheat. Virginia wheat withstood the long ocean voyage especially well. Alexandria's survival as a seaport was due to the fortunate change made by her planters and merchants soon after the middle of the eighteenth century from tobacco to wheat as their chief export product. The subsequent phenomenal growth and prosperity of the town was amazing.

A tobacco warehouse, a ferry, and a few scattered houses: this was all there was at Alexandria in 1740..

It was a good time to build a town in this vicinity. The Indians were no longer troublesome. The fort built of earth on the south side of Hunting Creek in 1676, to protect the earliest settlers, had crumbled away. As the Indians disappeared westward, the cultivated fields spread from the Potomac shore into the back country. Not all the crops belonged to the big landowners. The smaller plots were often worked by tenants or small landowners, some of whom had been indentured servants.

Before plantations grew so large that their owners had to depend on Negro slaves for the labor to work them, the indentured servant filled an important place in Virginia history. Hard times had put many men out of work in England. At the same time, there was a shortage of labor in America. Workmen were willing to leave home and cross the ocean, but usually did not have the money for even the cheapest ticket. Indentures solved the dilemma. By this system, actually a contractual agreement, a man gave a stipulated number of years of service, varying from two years to five years, in return for an advance for his passage.

Many indentured servants were skilled workmen. At Mount Vernon, the mantel in the family dining room was made by William Bernard Sears, an indentured servant. He also carved and gilded much of the interior of Pohick Church, where Washington was a vestryman and pew owner, and received fifty pounds nineteen shillings for the carving. An entry in the old Vestry Book reads:

> Ordered that William Bernard Sears gild the Ornaments within the Tabernacle Frames, the Palm Branch and Drapery on the front of the Pulpit, (also the Eggs on the Cornice of the small Frames if the Gold will hold out,) which he agreed to do for three pounds ready money, to be done with the Gold Leaf given to the Parish by Colo. George Washington.

The most famous indentured servant under contract to a plantation owner in the Alexandria vicinity was William Buckland, who was "a carpenter and joiner," and served George Mason. Gunston Hall, Mason's home on the Potomac, was the gathering place of the great men of the time. Buckland carved the magnificent interiors there, including the Chippendale Room, which is considered by many the finest of its kind in the United States. Buckland's four-year indenture stipulated that he would be provided with the necessary meat, drink, washing, and lodging, and would receive twenty pounds a year, payable quarterly.

The system of indentures obviously offered attractive advantages to those who participated in it. Its greatest disadvantage was that during the term an indentured servant was bound, he was as much the property of his master as a slave: he could be leased, or even

Indentured servants from England initially provided the specialized labor for Virginia plantations like Mount Vernon. Many were skilled craftsmen, such as William Bernard Sears who carved and gilded much of the interior of Pohick Church, Fairfax County, Va. (The exterior is pictured above.)

sold, to another master within the terms of his contract. However, when the period covered by his contract ended, he was once again a free man.

As the system of indentured servants continued in practice, it fostered a new and far-reaching unskilled labor problem. Vast amounts of land had been acquired by a handful of men as a result of fifty-acre headright grants. The more land a planter owned, the more laborers he needed to clear more and more fields for the soil-exhausting tobacco crops. At the same time, he kept losing the labor of indentured servants as they became free men. Eventually, the plantation owners tried to solve the problem by using Negro slave labor.

CHAPTER THREE

Alexandria's Early Settlers

Shortly before the town was founded, a number of agents representing Scottish import and export firms in Glasgow came up the Potomac River from Dumfries, a town some twenty-five miles to the south of Alexandria. These agents were in America chiefly to buy tobacco for their firms, and several of them were destined to play a prominent part in the early history of Alexandria. Outstanding were John Carlyle, William Ramsay and John Dalton, who arrived in 1740, in the same year if not actually together.

The newcomers settled around the warehouse on the Potomac. It was a pleasant location at the head of a mile-long arc whose almost perpendicular cliffs rose ten to fifteen feet above the Potomac River. It was near the head of tidewater with the Atlantic Ocean about two hundred miles away. Magnificent building sites with breath-taking views dotted the land for miles to the north and south. Today, the George Washington Masonic National Memorial stands on one of these. (According to tradition, Thomas Jefferson, Monticello's famous builder, had selected the Memorial site for the United States Capitol.)

House by house, a tiny hamlet grew up around the tobacco warehouse. The little community's single street was called Oronoco, so was the tobacco that grew in the vicinity, and a word very much like Oronoco was Algonquian for garden. The loyal Scottish residents named the settlement Belhaven, in honor of one of Scotland's heroes. They quickly realized that Belhaven offered possibilities for growth and the likelihood of becoming an important trading center. The harbor was adequate for ships of any size and the location was easily accessible to produce from the interior, so they initiated a campaign for supporters.

The idea of a new town spread swiftly and attracted the interest of residents in the outlying area. Fortunately, the promoters had powerful allies in two nearby planters, Lawrence Washington of Mount Vernon and Colonel William Fairfax of Belvoir, and the latter's cousin, Thomas, sixth Lord Fairfax and Baron of Cameron. He had recently come from England to make his permanent home in the colony. It was said that he left his native country because he had been disappointed in love. Temporarily, he was at Belvoir, the guest of his cousin.

Intermarriages between the Washington and Fairfax families and the would-be founders made the project for the new town almost a family affair. John Carlyle married one of Colonel Fairfax's daughters and Lawrence Washington married another. Mrs. William Ramsay was also related to the Washingtons.

The nearby plantations such as Mount Vernon provided great impetus to the development of Alexandria. George Washington and his half-brother, Lawrence, survey the Mount Vernon estate as it looked when Lawrence Washington was the owner.

These planters were astute businessmen. They knew that a seaport town near their plantations that would be a market center would benefit them as well as the merchants and others nearby who had commodities to buy and sell. So Lawrence Washington supported the petition in the General Assembly to establish the town at Hunting Creek on the Potomac River.

His action met with strong resistance. Most of the sixty acres of land proposed for the new town belonged to the Alexander family. The colonial government stipulated that this land should be laid out into lots; that the lots should be sold at auction; and that the Alexander heirs and other landowners be paid from the proceeds of the sale. John Alexander, a descendant and namesake of the early area landowner of that name, was a well-to-do merchant who lived on the family estate in another part of Virginia. He had inherited much of the property on which the new town was to be built. As he would have no control over the sale price of the lots, and of the monies that would come to him, he objected to having his holdings disposed of in this way.

To help him fight the petition, he supported a counter-petition. Both petitions were referred to the Committee of Propositions and Grievances. The Committee took under advisement Lawrence Washington's original petition and the counter-petition, which advocated a town located inland, at the head of Hunting Creek. Several months later, the Committee reported in support of Washington's site on the Potomac River. One provision of the act establishing the town gave absolute power to the twelve directors, or trustees, and to the successors whom they would name.

The Alexandria charter of 1748 is only about a thousand words long. Details were left to the trustees, to deal with as they arose. There were two definite restrictions: houses with wooden chimneys and swine running about freely were both prohibited. Years later the trustees were still trying to find effective laws that would keep homeowners and blacksmiths from building wooden chimneys, and enclosures strong enough to keep hogs within bounds at all times.

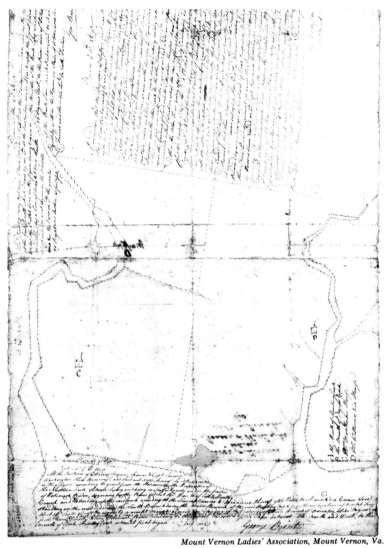

Mount Vernon Ladies' Association, Mount Vernon, Va.

In 1654, "Mistress Margaret Brent, Gentleman," received the land grant in Virginia that later became Alexandria. She was given the 700-acre grant on the Potomac River in exchange for bringing fourteen indentured servants to Virginia from England. Her brother, Giles Brent, and her infant nephew had grants below hers. Some of the Brent land, shown on the map above, was later purchased by George Washington for his Mount Vernon estate.

George Washington's first survey for the town of Alexandria, 1749.

"Land whereon stands the Town of Alexandria.

Note that on the bank fine cellars may be cut. From thence wharves may be extended on the flats without any difficulty and more houses built thereon as in Philadelphia. Good water may be got by sinking wells to small depth.

The above area of 51 acres 3 rods 31 perch belongs to:

 Capt. Philip Alexander
 Capt. John Alexander
 Mr. Hugh West.

The Shoals or Flats about 7 feet at high water."

32

CHAPTER FOUR

Alexandria Landowners

The story of Alexandria in recorded history goes back to 1654. The date has special significance for two reasons. It marks the year when the first private owner acquired the site of the future town. And it introduces Mistress Margaret Brent, Gent., the owner.

Mistress Brent was well known in Maryland for many years before then. Her name appears in that colony's court records a total of 124 times, as attorney for herself and in suits involving others over a period of thirteen years. Then, in 1654, she received a land grant in Virginia. This was the rectangular tract, containing 700 acres, on the Potomac River above Hunting Creek which almost a century later became the nucleus of Alexandria.

The Brent property line extended inland from the mouth of Hunting Creek in a westerly direction for a little less than a mile, roughly following the creek's shoreline. Turning northward, the boundary line ran parallel to the Potomac River for a mile. Then, proceeding eastward, it paralleled the first line along Hunting Creek. The course of this, the third side of the rectangle, came right through the middle of present-day Queen Street in Alexandria. At the Potomac River, this line extended southward for a mile to meet the beginning point.

(It was the custom in colonial days to grant fifty acres of land, known as a headright, for each inhabitant brought into Virginia. The grants were given in return for paying the passage of the men and women who emigrated to the New World. They, in turn, worked out the price of their passage over a period of years. By this method, the grantees, who were individuals of means, acquired vast amounts of land. Her 700-acre grant lists the names of the fourteen people she brought to Virginia.)

Margaret Brent was not only wealthy but also an Englishwoman of extraordinary ability. Some historians have called her the most powerful person in early Maryland, and she achieved this recognition despite the fact that women then were considered inferior to men and did not share equal rights with them. Margaret Brent fought this discrimination against her sex all her life. The title "Gent." indicates that she was at least partly successful.

The Brents, two sisters and two brothers, came to Maryland from England in 1638, with a retinue of maidservants and menservants. Margaret, a spinster, was about thirty-seven years old. She never married, but for many years was a close friend of Leonard Calvert, Governor of Maryland. When Lord Calvert lay dying, he named Margaret executrix of his estate before witnesses, telling her to "take all and pay all." Then, asking Margaret to remain at his bedside, he sent everyone else from the room so that their final farewell might take place in private.

After Lord Calvert's death, Margaret Brent came before the Maryland Council and asked for the right to vote as a member, both for herself as a landowner and as attorney and executor for Lord Calvert. The account of the proceedings reads that she was refused, and that she objected to the decision, surely one of the earliest official attempts of a woman to seek political equality for her sex in America.

No one knows just how strong a tie there was between Lord Calvert and Margaret Brent. It is known that they had more interests in common than business affairs. They even shared the joint guardianship of an Indian child. Together they formally and legally adopted the young daughter of the chief of the Piscataway Indians. Kittamaquund had left his little girl in the Brent household to be educated and reared as a Catholic. The child was baptized in 1642, when she was about nine years old, and at that time took the Christian name Mary for herself. Later, she married Margaret's brother, Giles. The story of Maryland's daughter of an Indian chief is so much like that of Virginia's Pocahontas that Mary Brent is known as the Maryland Pocahontas.

The Brent family was related to Lord Baltimore, the Proprietor of Maryland, but their blood ties did not prevent them from continually quarreling with him in public. Disagreements over land ownership caused many of their differences. Margaret Brent, in particular, suffered because of what she called Lord Baltimore's "disaffection" for her. The situation worsened and finally became so strained that the Brents decided to leave Maryland. Soon after Giles's marriage to the Indian chief's daughter, the Brent family crossed the Potomac

Margaret Brent, first owner of the land that now includes Alexandria, was probably the first feminist in Colonial America. Here she is petitioning the Maryland Council for the right to vote. The account of the proceedings tells she was turned down, and that she objected to the decision.

River and settled in Virginia, hopefully naming their new home Peace.

The earliest Virginia land grant made to a Brent was to Giles, in 1651. Then, in 1653, an entry in the Virginia land records lists Giles Brent, Jr., the year-old grandson of the "Emperor of the Piscataways," as owner of 800 acres on the Potomac. A century later George Washington added this same tract of land to his Mount Vernon estate. On September 6, 1654, Margaret Brent acquired the 700 acres above that owned by her infant nephew.

When Margaret died, she still owned this tract of land, the site of the town of Alexandria. Her will, written on December 26, 1663, begins with the customary enumeration of individual bequests. She left her niece Mary all six of her silver spoons. She ended the document with a sweeping flourish, characteristic of this amazing woman: ". . . to my brother Giles Brent and to his heirs forever I give all my lands, goods and chattles, and all my estate, real and personal, and all that is, or may be, due to me in England, Virginia, Maryland, or elsewhere . . ."

Six years after Margaret Brent wrote her will, a large tract of land in the same vicinity as hers was granted to Robert Howson for bringing 120 people to live in Virginia. His 6,000 acres began on the Potomac shore opposite and a little above where the Lincoln Memorial is today. The Brent and Howson grants were made fifteen years apart. They began at different points and ran in opposite directions. But the second grant overlapped and contained all of the first. Alexandria's site was included in both.

Robert Howson received his grant on October 21, 1669. Less than a month later, he sold the 6,000 acres to John Alexander for 6,000 pounds of tobacco and the

casks in which the tobacco leaf was packed. The two
men lived in Stafford County, Virginia, and were well-to-
do merchants. Alexander was also a surveyor. He had
surveyed the lands immediately below Howson's tract
for the Washington family earlier the same year, so he
knew the general area and apparently liked it. This
might explain his haste in buying the property from
Howson without making a survey. He soon ran into
ownership problems with Margaret Brent's heirs and
paid dearly for his oversight.

In the system of granting land then prevalent in
Virginia, there was no guarantee that the tract described
in the grant was not already within the bounds of a prior
grant. It was the responsibility of the applicant, not the
king or the proprietor, to rule out this possibility. As far
as is known, neither Robert Howson nor John Alexander
had checked to make certain that the Howson grant did
not conflict with an earlier grant.

Just how long a time elapsed before Alexander discovered that Margaret Brent was the prior owner of the
land included in his purchase from Howson is not
known. Nor is there any account on record of the negotiations between him and the Brent family, some of
whom were living in England. But an entry in the Virginia land records of January 14, 1674/5 notes that
John Alexander paid the Brent heirs 10,500 pounds of
tobacco and casks for their 700 acres. Obviously,
Alexander was in no position to bargain. He wanted the
choice riverfront section of land to which the Brent family held title and which he had presumed was his when
he paid Howson. So he had to pay for it a second time.
Under the circumstances, the Brents could and did set
the price. His original purchase from Howson had cost
Alexander only a pound of tobacco for an acre of land.
Now it cost him an additional fifteen pounds of tobacco

per acre for the 700 acres that Margarent Brent had owned.

The southernmost corner of the property was the same in each case. It is the bit of land jutting out into the river on Alexandria's boundary where Hunting Creek flows into the Potomac, now known as Jones Point. When President Washington selected the site for the Federal City, he named Jones Point in his proclamation designating the beginning of the ten mile square for the nation's capital. The Woodrow Wilson Bridge passes almost directly over the historic cornerstone marking the spot.

The site of the future town of Alexandria remained a wilderness for half a century after it was granted to Margaret Brent. The Indians were still such a menace in this vicinity in 1676 that the colonial government had built a fort nearby, a mile inland and on the south shore of Hunting Creek, for the settlers' protection. The cause for action then was the scalping of a young boy on the doorstep of his own home there. A few settlers built houses along the Virginia shore this far north by the early 1700's but even these fearless pioneers did not venture inland.

The precautions that the white men took to avoid any chance encounter with hostile Indians are clearly indicated in the descriptions of the boundaries in the land grants of that early period. The grantees reported their lines by reference to trees or rocks that they could have seen from the safety of their boats without ever setting foot on the Potomac shore. Most of these natural boundary markers disappeared in the course of time and, as a result, generations of descendants of the original owners were involved in lawsuits over property lines. This was so prevalent that foreigners traveling through the early settlements often made entries in their journals on the

The site of the future town of Alexandria was still very much menaced by Indians in 1676. The early settlers took elaborate precautions to avoid any chance encounters with hostile Indians. Often there was out-and-out conflict, however.

frequency with which Virginians went to court to settle their differences. Alexandria's early history abounds with such lawsuits.

A second reason for local boundary problems was due to transfer of ownership without surveying the land involved, as was the case with the Alexander land. George Washington and George Mason solved the problem of the boundary between Mount Vernon and Hollin Hall, the seat of Mason's son, Thomson, by erecting what Washington called in his will, ". . . double ditching with a post and rail fence thereon." The ditches were separated by a cleared space, and it was in the center of this, on top of the dirt that had been dug up from the ditches, that the fence was erected.

Leonard Calvert, who had been sent to Maryland by his brother, Lord Baltimore, to govern the colony.

CHAPTER FIVE

The Town Begins

As a friendly gesture to the Alexander family, the 1748 charter stipulated that the new town would be called by the name Alexandria. Some of the Scottish merchants living around the warehouse on the northern boundary of the new town were opposed to the new name and tried for years to restore the old name honoring their hero, Belhaven, but failed. A suburban community below Alexandria has revived that name although the spelling has been changed to Belle Haven.

The paper plans begun in 1748 finally materialized on July 13, 1749 when a public auction was held to sell lots. The Fairfax County surveyor, assisted by seventeen-year-old George Washington, had surveyed and laid off the sixty acres into lots and streets earlier that summer. Trees were probably chopped down so that the prospective purchasers and curious onlookers could more clearly visualize the ten streets of the neatly laid

43

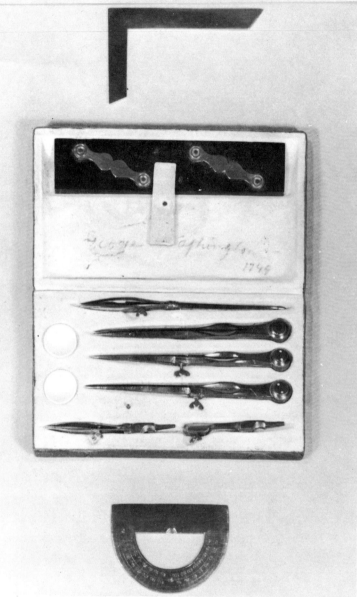

The "paper town" of Alexandria finally began to materialize when the Fairfax County surveyor, assisted by George Washington, surveyed and laid off the town's sixty acres into lots and streets early in the summer of 1749. A public auction to sell the lots was held on July 13, 1749. George Washington's surveying instruments—the tools of his trade—are here illustrated.

out gridiron plan for the town. The seven streets beginning at the river bank and extending westward were crossed at right angles by three streets parallel to the river. The town was divided into a total of eighty-four lots, four in each rectangular block. In the center of the town, one block was reserved for the Market Square, where, years later, Washington drilled his troops.

The street names show the founders' allegiance to England and to the double-titled Lord Fairfax, Baron of Cameron. Cameron Street bisects the town from east to west. The streets south of Cameron are King, Prince, and Duke. The streets north of Cameron are Queen, Princess, and—Oronoco. That street, officially named Duchess, leading to the tobacco warehouse on the Potomac, was originally the single street in the hamlet of Belhaven, and had been known as Oronoco. By 1749, this name was so familiar that the official name was never used, and the street is known as Oronoco to this day. Two of the streets crossing the town are Fairfax and Royal. The remaining one, fronting the Potomac, was named Water Street.

All of these street names are the same now as they were then, with the exception of Water Street. About a hundred years ago this street was renamed Lee Street in honor of General Robert E. Lee, who grew up in Alexandria. By that time, Water Street was no longer at the river's edge. The high bank had been cut down many years before for easier loading of the ships in the harbor. The project had added another full street, named Union, near the Potomac.

The northwest corner lot at the junction of Cameron and Water Streets was the first one put up for sale at the auction in 1749. John Dalton bought it for nineteen pistoles, a Spanish gold piece, valued at a trifle more than the English pound sterling. This is the first mention in

Library of Congress, Washington, D.C.

George Washington's plan for the town of Alexandria, 1749. The streets were divided into a total of eighty-four lots, four in each rectangular block.

the town's records of Dalton, the junior partner in the firm of Carlyle & Dalton, and a leading citizen of old Alexandria. It was not unusual that Dalton paid in pistoles. Then and for many years afterward there was a variety of foreign currency in use in the seaport town. One Alexandria lawyer's receipt lists "two Guineas weight two pounds, sixteen shillings & Ten pence, 13 round dollars, one French crown & a piece of Gold weight four pounds, ten shillings & four pence, in part of twenty-four pounds, as my fee . . ."

Dalton also bid successfully on an adjoining lot. Each purchaser was limited to two lots that first day of the sale in order to spread the ownership of the choicest lots among many and encourage the greatest number of residents. Pairs of lots were bought by several of the town's trustees, among them Colonel William Fairfax, his son George William Fairfax, Lawrence Washington, John Carlyle, and William Ramsay. The nearby planters were loyally supporting their newly-born market town. The four lots that Carlyle and Ramsay bought between them formed a full block. They faced the Potomac to the east and the Market Square to the west. They were unquestionably the choicest lots in the town. On the second, and last, day of the sale, Augustine Washington and George Mason also bought two lots apiece. Mason missed the chance to buy adjoining lots. However, when the original purchaser of the lot next to his defaulted, he consolidated his holdings by buying the intervening lot at a bargain price of only a few shillings.

A priceless Alexandria possession today is the original record book of the sale of the lots, containing the "Proceedings of the Board of Trustees . . . 1749-1767." The minutes of the meetings covering these years are on record in this book. So, also, are the payments made on the lots.

Building began all over town at once. Many Alexandria owners followed European precedent and their business was on the first, or street level, while the family

47

After the public auctioning of Alexandria's lots, building began at once. Many of the houses proudly featured a doubled drawing room, sometimes called a "ballroom," on an upper floor. Balls were important social events in the early life of the town.

lived in the floor, or floors, above. In a seaport market town a man's business had first place in his building plans, though many of these houses featured a double drawing room, sometimes called a ballroom, on an upper floor. The optimistic founders hoped to prosper and planned their homes accordingly. They provided the physical background for a future cultural and social center. When the capital city of Washington was putting up its first two public buildings, the Capitol and the President's House, representatives of the young republic happily exchanged the drab surroundings of their hotel or boarding house on The Hill to accept a dinner invitation in the beautiful home of a prosperous Alexandria merchant.

Ann Pamela Cunningham, the founder and first regent of the Mount Vernon Ladies' Association of the Union. She was the granddaughter of John Dalton of Alexandria, and when her mother was on a visit to Alexandria, she wrote home to Miss Cunningham at Rosemont Plantation, the family home in South Carolina, telling her of the deplorable condition of Washington's beloved Mount Vernon. As a result of this letter, the Association was formed that saved the historic estate for posterity.

CHAPTER SIX

Mount Vernon Plantation and Its Neighbors Belvoir and Gunston Hall

Ever since Captain John Smith's first glowing account of the beautiful Potomac River, the highly desirable riverfront land attracted many would-be owners. The river is navigable as far as the falls just above Washington and the earliest land grants stopped at this point. One ownership stipulation was the requirement to "plant or seat" the land within a specified time, usually three years. If the owner planted as little as one acre of a grant of thousands of acres, or built a hog pen instead of a house, he still met this requirement.

Even such token compliance was difficult along the last few miles of this upper region of the Potomac because of hostile Indians. One of the venturesome few who did secure title to land in this area was John Custis, the immigrant ancestor of Martha Washington's first husband, Daniel Parke Custis. The first Custis either lost or gave up his title to the land but a century and a half later John Parke Custis, Mrs. Washington's son, purchased land here again. George Washington Parke Custis, Mrs. Washington's grandson and Washington's ward, built Arlington House, now called the Custis-Lee Mansion, an early Greek Revival mansion with an excellent Doric portico. on part of this land. On the hillside above Arlington Cemetery, the house faces the Lincoln Memorial on the opposite side of the Potomac River.

One of the earliest riverfront land owners below Alexandria was George Washington's great-grandfather, John Washington. The Mount Vernon estate is on part of the original 2,500 acres that he acquired in 1674. It passed from one member of the family to another until it became the property of George's father, Augustine Washington. Before he owned it, he had leased it from his sister for a time and according to the terms of the lease he was to pay her "One Pepper Corn at the Feast of St. Michael the Arch Angel only if same be demanded." Augustine Washington brought his family to live at Epsewasson plantation, as it was then called, when George was about three years old. They stayed there only a short time, and after the father's death in 1743, George's half-brother, Lawrence, inherited the property. He changed its name to Mount Vernon, in honor of the British admiral under whom he served in the West Indies.

George Washington did a tremendous amount of work on the plantation, and its buildings, when he acquired it. No detail was too small for his attention. He even gave explicit directions for making the panelled pine boards on the outside walls for Mount Vernon. According to his instructions, the wood was laboriously cut and grooved by hand to resemble stone. Then the finish

Mount Vernon attracted so many visitors that Washington described it as "a well resorted tavern."

was applied by throwing sand on the wet paint. Washington called this a "rusticated board finish."

Fortunately, Washington's love for Mount Vernon, and his painstaking work on it, was not lost to posterity. It was a young lady from South Carolina, Ann Pamela Cunningham, who later saved the property. One day in

53

A view of Mount Vernon, showing the land side of the mansion and the river beyond. Beautiful trees and sweeping lawns characterized the estate then, as they still do today.

1853, she received a letter from her mother that read in part:

> It was a lovely moonlight night that we went down the Potomac. I went on deck as the bell tolled and we passed Mount Vernon. I was painfully distressed at the ruin and desolation of the home of Washington, and the thought passed through my mind: Why was it that the women of his country did not try to keep it in repair, if the men could not do it? It does seem such a blot on our country!

The young woman's reaction to her mother's idea was to write an appeal to the "Women of the South" urging them to contribute funds to purchase and preserve

Another early lithograph of farming at Mount Vernon. The view is from the river.

Washington's home. This was the beginning of The Mount Vernon Ladies' Association of the Union which to the present day holds Mount Vernon in trust dedicated to the memory of George Washington.

The reference to the bell tolling as the ship passed Mount Vernon is a custom that originated spontaneously shortly after Washington's death. One morning in May 1801, the crew of the *USS Congress*, which was on its way up the Potomac River to the navy yard in Washington, could clearly see Mrs. Washington and others of the

55

family on the portico of the mansion. The captain ordered the sails lowered, the flags displayed at half-mast, and a mourning salute of thirteen guns fired while the ship's company stood uncovered and motionless. Later, vessels adopted the custom of tolling a bell as they passed. President Theodore Roosevelt witnessed the bell ceremony and made it official for United States naval vessels when opposite Washington's tomb.

Five miles south and on a tract of about the same size as Mount Vernon was Belvoir, the plantation home of Colonel William Fairfax, the most influential man in this part of Virginia at that time. He was business agent for his cousin Thomas, sixth Lord Fairfax, the Proprietor of the Northern Neck of Virginia, and he was President of the Governor's Council, the second most important office in Williamsburg. Belvoir was built of brick and stood on an almost perpendicular bluff with a magnificent panoramic view of the Potomac River fifty feet below. There was a five-mile shoreline around the estate. The four rooms on the entrance floor of the house were divided by the wide central hallway characteristic of plantation houses. On the floor above were five bedrooms. The customary cluster of small outbuildings surrounded the mansion house.

The name Belvoir no longer recalls the family who lived there. Alexandria subscribers to the *Virginia Gazette* read a notice in the August 25, 1774 issue offering Belvoir for rent. The estate was described as a mansion house with outlying buildings; offices, stables, and coach house. Also, a garden, orchard, and several fisheries. The advertisement went on to say that anyone interested should see Colonel Washington who lived near it. The Belvoir furnishings were sold. Washington and some Alexandrians bought pieces of it. The house was destroyed by fire in 1783 and the blackened walls were completely demolished by the British in 1814. Today, the United States Army Engineer Center, Fort Belvoir, is located there. Thousands of people work and live at Fort Belvoir. In Alexandria, the large brick house at 207 Prince Street, known as the George William Fairfax House, is still a reminder of the Belvoir family and their connection with the town's early history.

Planters' homes are often spoken of as mansions. Actually, most plantation houses in the Alexandria neighborhood were unpretentious dwellings. Gunston Hall, the home of George Mason, is a story and a half house. And Mount Vernon, during most of George Washington's lifetime, was considerably smaller than it is today.

A few months after Lawrence Washington inherited Mount Vernon, he married Colonel Fairfax's daughter, Anne, and brought her to his estate. Eleven-year-old George was then living with his widowed mother. In the years that followed, he often came to stay at Mount Vernon, and sometimes visited his sister-in-law's family at Belvoir. Here he met Anne's brother, George William Fairfax, who was seven years his senior.

At sixteen, George Washington experienced surveying for the first time. Lord Fairfax engaged George William Fairfax to do some surveying for him, and young Washington went along to help. Shortly after the surveyors returned that fall of 1748, George Fairfax married Sally Cary and brought her to Belvoir.

Anne Washington was delighted to have Sally Fairfax at Belvoir and there was much visiting back and forth between the two estates. Sally Fairfax gave the boy George Washington his first opportunity to enjoy the companionship of a girl of about his own age. The

Photo by Charles Baptie, Annandale, Va. The Regents of Gunston Hall, Lorton, Va.
The home of George Mason: Gunston Hall, river view, Lorton, Va. Colonial Virginia planters like George Mason were men of varied talents, and designing houses and supervising their construction were among the planters' duties. Mason had the brick for Gunston Hall made on the estate, and there are written records showing how specific he was about the measurements for lime and sand.

friendship between the two that began then continued as long as they lived, even though during most of it they were separated by the Atlantic Ocean. At the time of the American Revolutionary War, the Fairfaxes left America to make their home in England, and never returned.

At about the time George and Sally Fairfax married, another newcomer joined Alexandria's plantation families. George Mason came to live at Dogue Neck, his plantation five miles below Belvoir. The Dogue Neck estate was twice as large as either Mount Vernon or Belvoir, and reached so far out into the Potomac River that it was almost an island. It needed only a mile of fencing to keep the tame deer that roamed freely on the estate from rejoining the herd in the wilderness surrounding it. The Dogue Neck peninsula was part of George Mason's inheritance.

George Mason, the fourth of that name in Virginia, is known in history as George Mason of Gunston Hall. He was probably known at one time as the wealthiest boy in Virginia, possibly in all colonial America. One day as the third George Mason was crossing the Potomac to the Maryland plantation where the family was living, the boat capsized in a sudden squall and he drowned. He had made no will and by the law of primogeniture his eldest son, ten-year-old George, inherited all his estate.

The widowed Mrs. Mason took her three young children to Chappawamsic, her dower plantation in Virginia. Chappawamsic was considerably south of Alexandria, inland and virtually at the edge of civilization. Only a few years before this, Governor Alexander Spotswood of Virginia had arranged with the friendly Indians near Chappawamsic to bring runaway slaves to the Mason plantation. They would receive a gun or two blankets in exchange. At this point in the negotiations, according to tradition, the Governor unpinned a golden horseshoe that he was wearing and gave it to the Indian interpreter.

The little horseshoe was the emblem of the Knights of the Golden Horseshoe. George Mason's father is said

Mrs. Seymour St. John, Wallingford, Conn.

Sally Cary Fairfax (Mrs. George William Fairfax), by Duncan Smith. George
Washington wrote to Mrs. Fairfax from Camp at Fort Cumberland, Md.,
"'Tis true, I profess myself a votary of love. I acknowledge that a lady is
in the case, and further confess that this lady is known to you. Yes, madam,
as well as she is to one who is too sensible to her charms to deny the
power whose influence he feels and must ever submit to." ("Writings of
Washington" edited by John C. Fitzpatrick.)

to have been a member of this little band of cavaliers on
their mountain expedition of discovery in the summer of
1716. Governor Spotswood and about fifty men, some of

them forest rangers and Indian guides, left Williamsburg to explore the territory beyond the Blue Ridge Mountains. Well equipped and in gay humor they rode through the wilderness. Each day they hunted or fished for their meals, and each night they camped out under the stars after a feast of good food and fine wines. In two weeks they reached the summit of the mountains and looked down at the beautiful scene that stretched for miles in every direction. Descending to the valley, Governor Spotswood took possession of all they had discovered in the name of the king. Then he put a formal document attesting to this in a bottle, from the contents of which they had toasted the various members of the ruling family, and buried it beside the Shenandoah River.

When they returned home, the Governor is said to have presented his companions with horseshoe-shaped gold ornaments. The mementos are described as decorated on one side with precious stones representing nailheads and with an inscription on the reverse side, *Sic juvat transcendere montes* (Thus it helps to cross the mountains). The little golden horseshoes symbolized the expedition over the rocky mountains with frequent stops to re-shoe the horses because of the rough terrain.

George Mason probably heard this story many times during the years he lived at Chappawamsic. About 1746, soon after his twenty-first birthday, he left his mother's house and selected the plantation of Dogue Neck, south of the future town of Alexandria, for his own home. Four years later, he married sixteen-year-old Ann Eilbeck, the only child of a well-to-do Maryland family. The Eilbeck plantation, Mattawoman, was near the Mason home where the family was living when George's father drowned. The Eilbecks and Masons were long-time neighbors and old friends: George had known his bride since she was two years old. The newly wed couple crossed the Potomac to begin their married life at Dogue Neck. Here they built Gunston Hall.

The Virginia planter was a man of varied capabilities. For some, like George Mason, designing a house and supervising its construction to the smallest detail were part of the normal activities connected with running a plantation.

The brick for Gunston Hall was made on the estate. George Mason was very specific about the measurements of lime and sand, stipulating the different proportions of each to be used in the mortar mixed for indoor and outdoor work. He wrote to a friend warning him against including clay or loam in the mix:

> I wou'd by no means put Clay or Loam in any of the Mortar. In the first place the Mortar is not near so strong and besides from its being of a more soft and crumbly nature, it is very apt to nourish and harbour those pernicious little vermin the Cockroaches. . . . I have seen some brick Houses so infested with these Devils that a Man had better have lived in a Barne than in one of them.

Ann Eilbeck Mason (Mrs. George Mason), companion portrait to that of her husband painted by Boudet after the lost Hesselius.

George Mason, painted by D. W. Boudet in 1811 after the lost original done from life by John Hesselius in 1750, the year of Mason's marriage. Mason was the author of the first Ten Amendments to the Constitution of the United States (known as the Bill of Rights).

CHAPTER SEVEN

The Life of the Planter

Alexandria's plantation neighbors bought property in the town and exchanged visits with Alexandrians, so the townspeople came to know the planters intimately. They knew that a planter's day was crowded with responsibilities. They seldom saw him come to town just for pleasure, although they might do their business with a merchant early in the day and dine with friends or go to the theatre that night.

Planters had to be astute businessmen. The crops they raised were their merchandise. Tobacco, and later wheat, were the chief export crops of the plantations in the Alexandria neighborhood. Washington was one of the first planters in this area to turn to wheat. The soil at Mount Vernon did not produce a good tobacco crop; wheat, and the flour made from wheat, proved more profitable. Mason, too, grew large crops of wheat. It is said that he shipped 23,000 bushels of wheat from his own wharf at one time. There was a market for all the wheat that the planters near Alexandria could grow.

Corn was the food crop, with fish second in importance. All life on the plantation lived on corn. Since the normal yield from a field of Indian corn was twenty times that of a field of wheat, cornmeal was used in place of flour for almost everything except pie crust. Corn fed the cattle that provided the food for the slaves who planted the corn to feed the cattle.

Crop raising was only one of the planter's major responsibilities. A plantation was a self-sustaining community and the entire population was completely dependent on the man who lived in the mansion house. There were about 300 slaves at Mount Vernon and 500 at Gunston Hall. It took a large number of them just to produce the essential food, shelter and clothing for their own people. Some were taught skilled trades. These were the carpenters, blacksmiths, tanners, shoemakers, weavers, etc. Some were trained as house servants. But the great majority of them worked in the plantation fields, raising the chief crops.

The planter was his own efficiency expert and kept a record of everything connected with running his plantation. He listed each worker by name and the particular task that he performed at a given time, and spent long hours at his books. Letters and orders were handwritten, with copies made and filed.

Occasionally, a planter's son or the son of a friend helped with this writing task. George Washington Craik, the son of Washington's physician, Dr. James Craik of Alexandria, did such clerical work at Mount Vernon. At one time, there were two other Washington namesakes there: George Washington Parke Custis, Mrs. Washington's grandson, and George Washington Louis Gilbert

Mount Vernon Ladies' Association, Mount Vernon, Va.

Dr. James Craik's desk, a gift from George Washington. The two men were close friends, and the desk was in Dr. Craik's Alexandria home for many years. It is now at Mount Vernon.

Motier de Lafayette, the Marquis de Lafayette's only son, who was on a visit to America.

At Gunston Hall, Mason's sons often helped with his writing. During the days and sometimes weeks when he was at work on the documents for which he became famous, hardly anyone in the family except these older sons talked with him between meals. The other children (he had nine) might catch a glimpse of him when he left his desk briefly to walk in his garden, pacing back and forth along the box-bordered path, deep in thought. At such times he wore a little cap, white linen in summer and green velvet in winter, on his cleanly shaven head. He shaved it himself, twice weekly. The luxuriant, dark, wavy hair seen framing Mason's face in his portrait was a wig. He had several wigs and always kept one handy on a stand near his desk. When wigs went out of fashion, Mason stopped shaving his head and grew a thick "suit" of hair.

Mason always joined his family for dinner in the middle of the day. One of his older sons usually prepared his customary bowl of toddy, and the two would go through a playful ritual. Before accepting the drink, Mason said, "I pledge you, Sir." Then the boy put his lips to the rim of the bowl before handing it to his father. Mason explained to his sons that this custom originated during the troubled times in England when a man's drink was sometimes poisoned by enemies within his own house, making it necessary for him to take the precaution of asking the one who prepared it to drink first. At the table, Mason said grace, and always used the same words: "God bless us, and what we are going to receive."

Washington's day began early. He also did considerable writing and visited activities around the mansion before breakfast. At Mount Vernon this meal was served at about seven o'clock. After breakfast Washington rode out on horseback to inspect his farms and returned in time to dress for dinner at three. On Sunday guests would accompany the family home from church. Plantation houseguests came often and stayed long. Their host frequently spent the hours between dinner and the light supper meal entertaining them. Many of the plantations in the Alexandria neighborhood were on or near the direct road from north to south, the historic post road, part of which is now U.S. Route No. 1. One Virginia planter who lived on this much-travelled road found it inconvenient to hold open house continuously and actually built a house at a less accessible spot rather than turn guests from his door.

Mount Vernon attracted so many visitors that Washington described it as "a well resorted tavern." As the years passed visitors increased, and the Washingtons were alone so rarely that Washington wrote: "Mrs. Washington & myself will do what I believe has not been done within the last twenty Years by us, that is to set down to dinner by ourselves."

One day two rain-drenched riders arrived at Mount Vernon. They were Bushrod Washington, a nephew and the heir to Mount Vernon, and John Marshall, the great Chief Justice of the United States and Washington's first biographer. When they reached into the single pair of saddlebags they shared for convenience, they pulled out a bottle of whiskey, a twist of tobacco, some cornbread, and rough clothing. At some tavern along the 100-mile trip from Richmond they had mistakenly exchanged saddlebags with a wagon-driver, and the clothes that the Mount Vernon guests unpacked belonged to the workman. Washington roared with laughter at their predicament and sympathized with the wagoner, who

Like the other Colonial Virginia planters, George Washington's day began early. He often rode out in the early morning to inspect his farms. Here, in a detail from an 1853 lithograph after a painting by Junius Brutus Stearns, Washington is shown as a farmer. The Mount Vernon mansion is seen in the far background.

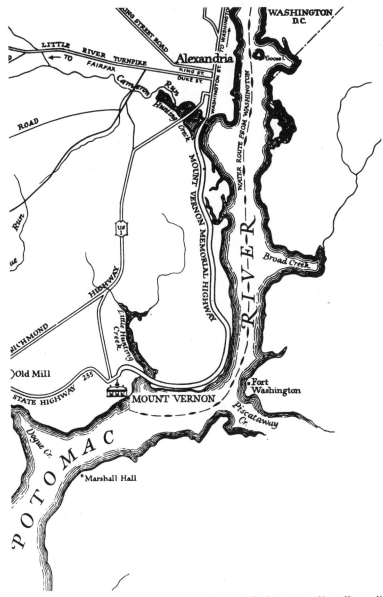

Mount Vernon Ladies' Association, Mount Vernon, Va.

Mount Vernon, like many of the other plantations in the Alexandria neighborhood, was on the historic north-south post road, now part of U.S. Route No. 1.

71

Mount Vernon Ladies' Association, Mount Vernon, Va.
Many portraits have been made of Martha Washington, George Washington's wife. Among the most famous is this miniature by the well-known early American artist, Charles Willson Peale.

would have to wear the lawyers' knee breeches and frock coats.

Gunston Hall also had its share of guests. Thomas Jefferson was a frequent visitor and in a letter to Mason wrote that whenever he passed the Gunston Hall gate, he would give himself the pleasure of turning in. The Bill of Rights, the first ten amendments to the Constitution, are based on the Declaration of Rights that Mason drew up for Virginia in May and June of 1776. They contain a body of rules protecting the inherent rights of man that Mason thought are a man's birthright because he is a human being. They begin by guaranteeing the right of petition, of freedom of religion, of speech, and of the press.

Mason was always available to the men who stopped at Gunston Hall to talk with him. At times, Mrs. Mason felt the lack of privacy in her home. As the colonies moved closer to the break with England, and more and more of the leading men came to confer with Virginia's great thinker, Mrs. Mason, who was expecting her seventh child, left Gunston Hall in search of seclusion. She had herself rowed across the Potomac River to await the birth at her parents' home.

Besides entertaining visitors and visiting in turn, the nearby planter and his wife enjoyed Alexandria's recreational attractions. The theatre was a favorite. The plays at Gadsby's Tavern, and at a little theatre called Liberty Hall, were well attended. Dancing was popular. Fiddlers provided the music for these gatherings. Traveling dancing masters taught the younger children. The Mount Vernon children were brought to Gunston Hall for their dancing lessons when the dancing master came there, and vice versa.

The Virginia planter's chief at-home recreation centered around his horses. He imported and bred splendid animals, and was very proud of them. He enjoyed fox hunting and horse racing. Alexandria had its own Jockey Club, and Washington is said to have been a member. Colonial women, riding sidesaddle, created charming pictures in the trailing, full skirts of their riding habits. The little Negro boy perched behind them, clinging to the horse, had a job to do. At each gate, he slid down from the horse, opened the gate to let his mistress ride through, and then hurriedly shutting the gate, ran and pulled himself back up on his perch to ride to the next gate. Mrs. Mason loved to ride, and her children named their mother's riding crop "the green doctor" because she used it so effectively in disciplining them. Occasionally, the women joined the men in events featuring horses. Cards were also enjoyed by many, and Washington sometimes played a game of whist before retiring at nine o'clock.

After a strenuous day of supervising activities at Mount Vernon, and entertaining the many guests who stopped off at the plantation, George Washington often enjoyed a good game of whist before retiring at nine o'clock. This is the card table at Mount Vernon.

The William Ramsay House. It was the first house in Alexandria to be built after the 1749 auctioning off of the town's lots. Ramsay was a prominent Alexandria merchant, who was related to George Washington by marriage.

CHAPTER EIGHT

A Paper Town Becomes Real

When the two day auction ended at the close of business that July 14, 1749, most of the lots in the new town of Alexandria had been sold. The first house completed was built by William Ramsay. Broad shouldered and with the ruddy coloring of a Scotsman, Ramsay bought and sold merchandise varying from a yard of black crepe for a new widow to half a shipload of bushels of wheat and barrels of flour. He was also a very active entrepreneur in real estate. His marriage to Anne Ball McCarty, a relative of George Washington's mother, was an important social asset.

Alexandria's Scottish residents elected a Lord Mayor on November 30, 1761. The members of the St. Andrew's Society, a Scottish benevolent organization, bestowed this honor on William Ramsay and invested him with a gold chain and medal. The newly elected Lord Mayor, preceded by sword and mace bearers, marched in the grand procession headed by a band and flags. Marchers on foot and on horseback joined in the merrymaking. The sidewalks and the rooftops were crowded with people. The ships riding at anchor in the harbor unfurled their flags and the noise from their guns added to the pandemonium. The townspeople ignored the fact that Alexandria was governed by a self-perpetuating Board of Trustees and that there was no official sanction from the royal government in Williamsburg for electing a Lord Mayor. Some of the leading citizens marched in the procession with Ramsay, his Aldermen, and the Common Council, and joined them later at the Coffee House and at a ball in the evening.

Ramsay's house shared a block with what was then the finest house in Alexandria, John Carlyle's manor-like mansion, set well back from Fairfax Street. It is reminiscent of river plantation estates in Virginia and, like them, may have had smaller buildings on each side connected to the main house. The wide central hallway of the imposing masonry house, open to Fairfax Street on the land side, lead to the gardens and a view of the Maryland shore across the Potomac River. Fine Madeira wine and other luxuries were unloaded directly from Carlyle's ships through the brick-walled, tunnel-like entrance in the garden to the storage spaces beneath the house.

One of the four rooms on the entrance floor of the Carlyle House is known as the Blue Room. When Major General Edward Braddock arrived in Alexandria from England, he held a council in this room with five colonial governors to discuss plans for the French and Indian War. The question of financing the expedition arose, and the royal governors suggested taxing the colonies. From this, Alexandrians claim that the first step toward war

The Carlyle House is architecturally like river plantations in southern Virginia. The small building on the left later housed the first bank of Alexandria.

The Carlyle House, river view. The back of the house faced handsome gardens and a view of the Maryland shore across the Potomac River.

"The Blue Room," Carlyle House. It was in this room that General Edward Braddock held his first council to discuss plans for the French and Indian War.

with Great Britain and the independence of the American colonies took place in their town.

Carlyle's property was separated from that of his partner in the import-export merchant business, John Dalton, by Cameron Street. Dalton, too, owned half a block of riverfront property. And as Ramsay and Carlyle had done, he built his house facing Fairfax Street.

Dalton, the purchaser of the first lot sold in Alexandria, was also the first man appointed by the charter member trustees of Alexandria when a vacancy occurred. He was a friend of Washington's, and the two men often visited one another. There is a dormer-windowed room in Dalton's house that is pointed out as the one Washington sometimes occupied. Dalton's claim to fame is connected with Washington but comes through his great-granddaughter, Ann Pamela Cunningham.

Ramsay, Carlyle, Dalton and other private owners of lots were joined in their construction projects by public buildings. George Mason headed the Fairfax County residents who, together with many Alexandrians, petitioned to have the county courthouse moved to the new town in 1752. The courthouse and prison were to be built with funds raised by subscription and lottery. Alexandria's trustees had no power to raise funds for this purpose through taxes, etc. When the people's petition was approved, they put up notices of a public lottery, offering prizes for lucky numbers. With the money they raised, they built the courthouse on the Market Square.

One of the first legal documents brought to the new courthouse was Lawrence Washington's will. It had been witnessed by John Dalton and was presented for probate by the executors, John Carlyle, Colonel George Fairfax, George William Fairfax, and George Washington. By the terms of the will, Lawrence Washington's "lots in Alexandria and the edifices thereon" were to be sold to pay his debts. Two years later, his half-brother, George, rented Mount Vernon from Lawrence's widow, who had a life interest in it, and when she died in 1761, George Washington acquired title to the plantation.

Court days in old Alexandria were very much like a theatre play. A kaleidoscope of scenes would pass before the people on a typical day in court, such as this one when George Mason and four other gentlemen justices held court. On a debt owed for ten years, the court orders the defendant to make payments on it until the debt, interest, and court costs are paid in full. Sheriff William Ramsay brings action against John Dalton and other of his assistants for failing to render their accounts. The assistants argue that this does not constitute a debt. Case is dismissed. Ramsay moves to the other side of the courtroom and takes his place as a gentleman justice among the others on the bench. In rapid succession, the court listens to a report from a committee regarding a road to a new church, appoints two men to repair a bridge, grants a license for an inn, appoints a guardian for a minor, and orders a boy to be apprenticed to a cooper under the care of the parish churchwardens, who are to see that the youngster is taught how to make barrels and to read and write. Then the case of a cabinetmaker versus the court clerk comes up. Although the cabinetmaker had made the two walnut bookcases ordered in a satisfactory manner, he had been unable to collect payment from the court clerk. The accused man's head sinks lower and lower over his desk, his pen quill shaking, while the audience laughs. The banging of the gavel finally restores order and the session continues.

On occasion, the principals in these colonial Alexandria courtroom scenes played their parts with finesse. One quaint custom was to use carefully chosen fictitious names, a variation of modern hidden persuasion methods. When John Carlyle filed suit against one member of the Alexander family, he did so as Aminadab Seekright; the defendant's name was Timothy Dreadnaught.

Justice was dispensed both inside and outside the courthouse. The pillory and whipping post had their places on the Market Square outside. One day the passersby saw a most gruesome sight. On pikes surrounding the courthouse chimney were the heads of several slaves who had been caught plotting to kill their overseers.

Entire families came to town from the country on court days in Alexandria, just as they do for town meeting in New England. Fair days often coincided with court days, and the farmer's wife selected her best preserves to display in the Market Square. She also brought some of her finest linen cloth, made from homegrown flax. The men organized cock fights. Local laws were relaxed so that everyone could have a good time. All persons were exempt from arrest for civil offenses beginning two days before and extending two days after a fair.

Business profits jumped during fair days. Deals involving large sums of money were transacted in tobacco notes. Pocket money in small denominations was scarce in early Alexandria. The people solved this by simply cutting coins into sections. The sharp and jagged edges of these pie-shaped coins were called sharpshins. They often cut their way through the men's pockets. So many were lost in this way in the alley leading from the Market Square to a nearby inn favored by hucksters and wagoners that it was named Sharpshin Alley.

CHAPTER NINE

A Travel and Military Center

Alexandria attracted a large number of people because of its geographic position on the direct route from
north and south. When John Pagan, one of the original
trustees, planned to leave America and advertised his
lots in Alexandria for sale, he pointed out that they were
located where four of the then existing seven public
roads in the colony crossed. An inn was essential for
those who traveled these roads. The City Tavern, one of
the first public buildings erected in Alexandria, filled
this need.

In Virginia, these forerunners of modern motels
were called ordinaries, a name that gave foreign tourists
a chance to poke fun at them. No doubt, frontier accommodations in the New World compared unfavorably
with the old established inns in Great Britain or Europe.
Guests often had to sleep dormitory fashion, in one large
room, in America's public houses and if they wanted

"Link boys"—the counterparts of our modern bus boys—meet a guest in a typical colonial tavern courtyard.

Photo by Marler, Alexandria.

Architecturally, the City Tavern (left) is said to be the finest surviving inn built in colonial times. It was constructed in 1752. Forty years later a larger building, the City Hotel (right) was added to it. Together, they are known as Gadsby's Tavern.

fresh sheets had to pay extra for them. Travelers from abroad complained in particular of the system of serving meals at set times, the American hotel plan of today. But they seldom complained of the food itself. Virginia hams were a luxury export product and were the delight of connoisseurs everywhere, and the seaport town of Alexandria could supply the finest in native foods and imported luxuries.

Architecturally, the City Tavern, with its magnificently carved wooden doorway, is said to be one of the finest surviving inns built in colonial times. Alexandria's oldest inn, also known as the Coffee House, was built in 1752. Forty years later a larger building, the City Hotel, was added to it and both came under the management of John Gadsby. Although he never owned them, his hospitality made them so world famous that they are still called Gadsby's Tavern.

Alexandria was still mainly concerned with matters relating to building a town when, just five years after it was created, the upsetting news arrived from Williamsburg that French Canadians were in the Ohio Valley. Governor Robert Dinwiddie feared this threat to England's claim to that region and decided to send a force there to put a stop to any French plans. He named Alexandria as headquarters, appointed Carlyle as Commissary of Supply for the expedition, and instructed Washington, who had recently returned from an exploratory trip to the French camp, to recruit and train the assembled men in Alexandria.

Washington spent most of the month of March 1754 in the town. During the day, he drilled his slowly increasing force of recruits in the Market Square. In the evening, the twenty-two-year old Lieutenant Colonel relaxed. He had had some new shirts made up recently. On March 22, he stopped at William Ramsay's store on the corner of King and Fairfax Street and charged a pair of "white glazed lamb gloves" to his account, perhaps to wear to a dance at Gadsby's. Then on the night before he left Alexandria with his troops, he made another purchase at Ramsay's. Now his thoughts were evidently on the problems he would be facing in the field. He bought sixteen-and-a-half gallons of rum, the incentive drink and also, when needed, the anesthetic substitute.

On April 2, riding in front of his first command of 120 fighting men, Washington headed westward out of Alexandria. In the company was the town's physician-surgeon, Dr. James Craik, who that day began the close association with Washington that lasted until Washington died, when Dr. Craik stood at his bedside.

The expedition that spring of 1754 ended in a victory for the French. In London, the reaction to the news of Washington's defeat was the appointment of Major General Edward Braddock as commander of a force to be sent to North America. Again Alexandria was chosen as headquarters.

Events were spaced far apart in the days when it took four months to cross the Atlantic Ocean, and a year passed. The following spring, Alexandrians crowded the waterfront to gaze in wonder at the thirteen British transports and three ordnance ships that filled their harbor. They watched as the important men came ashore led by Braddock who was followed by Commodore Augustus Keppel, commander of His Majesty's squadron, and accompanied by Governor Robert Dinwiddie of Virginia. Major John Carlyle, Commissary of Supply for the Virginia forces, invited them to make his house their headquarters as they waited for the other colonial governors to arrive for a council of war. It was then that Washington met Braddock and was invited to join the British general's military family.

The troops pitched camp on the outskirts of Alexandria, about where Christ Church now is, and unloaded the ships. It was an unseasonably early hot and humid Virginia spring and the men, who were unaccustomed to such weather, grumbled. A thousand barrels of beef put on board in December were unfit to use and caused more grumbling. A thousand soldiers encamped in a town of less than half that number of inhabitants created special problems. With little to do as they waited for marching orders, the men took to drinking heavily and strict disciplinary measures, with even death as a penalty, were invoked.

Women had also come with the troops. They were laundresses, nurses, and wives. Braddock's commissary officer had even brought with him his widowed sister, Mrs. Charlotte Browne, who kept a diary of the expedition. Of her five-week stay in Alexandria, she wrote that the best accommodation that she could find in the overcrowded town was a tiny room with a single piece of furniture, the bed. She was sitting on this, sewing on her "tilt," the canopy that would turn her wagon into a bedroom when the army moved westward, when Mrs. Carlyle came to call and sent her servant home for chairs. While Mrs. Browne was in Alexandria, she was invited to a memorial service. She found both the widow and her house draped in yards and yards of black crepe, and noted with surprise the custom of burying the deceased in their own gardens. Mrs. Browne, too, complained of that extremely hot May, which she wrote turned her room into a steamy bath-house and left her exhausted after boiling hams and baking bread to take along on the march. In addition, she was upset because she had to discharge her maid for petty stealing.

At last, four provincial governors arrived. Horatio Sharpe of Maryland, William Shirley of Massachusetts,

James DeLancey of New York, and Robert Morris of Pennsylvania met with Braddock at his headquarters, the Carlyle House. Alexandria, which suddenly found itself host to the leading men of the country, burst with excitement. The resplendent officials, attended by aides and servants, drew crowds whenever they appeared. The idle and curious gathered in the Market Square to watch the red-coated guards at their posts in front of the Carlyle House, and generations of Alexandrians heard tales of the events then taking place.

Even as Braddock and the royal governors were holding their council of war, a regiment was already on the march. They left many of the heavy cannon that they had brought from England in Alexandria. It would have been difficult to transport them through the wilderness under the best of conditions but a sudden wet snowfall made the freshly cleared, stump-filled roads leading out of town impassable. Some of the cannon have been preserved in Alexandria as mementos. One forms the central support for a fountain in the Tavern Square. Another stands guard at the Alexandria end of the road named in Braddock's honor.

Braddock was defeated and lost his life in the battle against the French and Indians. The English losses were terrific. More than half of the twelve or thirteen hundred men in action were either killed or wounded, including almost every officer. Thus it fell to George Washington, who had miraculously escaped unscratched, to read the service at Braddock's burial. Because he feared that the Indians would discover the grave and mutilate the corpse, he ordered the troops and wagons to pass over the spot to hide every trace of the mound. The legends of Washington the soldier began at that battle in July, 1755.

Detail from *Braddock's Defeat*, by Edwin Willard Deming. The painting depicts General Braddock, mortally wounded, falling from his horse. The English losses were awesome. Leading the troops who limped back to Alexandria was George Washington, who luckily escaped injury.

The surviving Alexandrians returned home. Washington, although anxious to reach Mount Vernon which he had only recently acquired, took time to stop at the Carlyle House and deliver a message from one of Braddock's wounded aides, who had left his belongings there. Mrs. Browne's brother died in the wilderness and she sailed for England with her diary.

Photo by Marler, Alexandria, Va.

A fire place wall detail at 601 Duke Street, Alexandria.

CHAPTER TEN

An Era of Growth

Life in Alexandria returned to normal. Trade continued to grow rapidly, as did shipbuilding, ropemaking, and other activities of a seaport town. Wheat export lead all other commodities. The British navy in the West Indies was Alexandria's best flour customer. Alexandria prospered and by 1762 new streets were added to the town.

While the build-within-two years stipulation was in force, a lot owner's failure to comply cost him his property. His loss might be the next buyer's gain, as had been the case with George Mason. But this was usually the exception as property values increased rapidly in the town. Augustine Washington, George's half-brother, paid fifteen pistoles for two lots when he bought them at the original sale. Five years later, he lost them because he had not built on them. Then William Ramsay paid thirty-six and a half pistoles for them.

The two-year building requirement may be the reason for one form of Alexandria architecture. This is the flounder house. No one seems to know why so many of these oddly-shaped narrow half-houses, split down the middle, were built in early Alexandria, but there are various suppositions. The tallest side of these flat houses is windowless, like the sightless side of the flounder fish, and hence their name. One reason given for the wall without windows is that glass was expensive and subject to an import tax. And because flounder houses are always set back from the street, with the long blind wall on the lot line, it is said that they were put up as an ell to meet the time stipulation but that the main house was never built. Had a similar house, reversed, been built on the adjoining lot, they would have made quite a handsome structure, with a common wall on the lot line and the gable end to the street. The manse, now the educational building, of the Presbyterian Meeting House is an example of a flounder house.

Three churches associated with Alexandria's early history and with its plantation neighbors were built almost simultaneously and were completed in consecutive years. Pohick Church south of Alexandria was built in 1772; Christ Church in 1773; and the Presbyterian Meeting House in 1774. St. Mary's Catholic Church was built later, in 1795, and was the first permanent Catholic church in Virginia. All these churches have Washington associations: he was a vestryman of Pohick Church for twenty-two years; he purchased a pew at Christ Church the year it was built; he was present at the organizational meeting and contributed to the building fund of St. Mary's Church; and because the December weather made walking difficult along the then unpaved streets to Christ Church when he died in 1799,

Photo by William C. Arnold, Alexandria

A unique form of Alexandria architecture is "the flounder house." Why
these oddly-shaped, narrow half-houses were built still remains a mystery.
The tallest side of the houses were always windowless, like the sightless
side of a flounder fish. A fire mark, or fire plaque, is above and to the
left of the door, and indicates the owner of the home was insured for fire.
These plaques are also distinctive Alexandria landmarks.

Photo by Marter, Alexandria.

The Washington Street entrance to the churchyard, Christ Church, Alexandria.

Christ Church, Alexandria, from the Parish House.

An old engraving of Christ Church, Alexandria.

George Washington purchased this pew at Christ Church, the year it was built (1773). It shows the simple, yet handsome, designs of early Virginia church interiors.

The gold lettering on the tablets in Christ Church is original, never having needed retouching since the church was built in 1773. Photograph detail shows one of the two tablets with the original gold lettering that are on either side of the pulpit.

102

The Presbyterian Meeting House, Alexandria. The memorial service for George Washington was held here because bad weather made it too difficult to walk to Christ Church.

The entrance to the Presbyterian Meeting House, Alexandria.

104

The Unknown Soldier of the American Revolutionary War. The inscription on this tomb in the churchyard of the Presbyterian Meeting House reads: "Here lies a soldier of the Revolution whose identity is known but to God. His was an idealism that recognized a supreme being, that planted religious liberty on our shores, that overthrew despotism, that established a people's government, that wrote a Constitution setting metes and bounds of delegated authority, that fixed a standard of value upon men above gold and lifted high the torch of civil liberty along the pathway of mankind. In ourselves his soul exists as part of ours, his memory's mansion."

An old engraving of St. Mary's Catholic Church, Alexandria.

Photo by Wm. Edmund Barrett, Clifton, Va.

St. Mary's Catholic Church, Alexandria, today.

The Marquis de Lafayette stood at the doorway of this' house at 601 Duke Street to greet the Alexandrians who had come to honor him when he made his final tour of the United States in 1824. The diminutive Frenchman, who was staying at the house on the opposite side of the street, mounted these steps in order to see the citizens of Alexandria and be seen by them.

Mr. and Mrs. John Howard Joynt
Photo by Chas. Baptie, Annandale, Va.

A view of the hallway at 601 Duke Street showing the magnificently carved woodwork of this lovely home in old Alexandria.

his memorial service was preached at the Presbyterian Meeting House.

The inscriptions on many of the gravestones in these old churches in the Alexandria area are capsules of history. Long Tom, a chief of the Doeg Indians, is buried at Pohick Church. Thirty-four Confederate soldiers, prisoners of war who died in Federal hospitals in Alexandria, rest under one mound in the churchyard at Christ Church. It is believed that the oldest gravestone in St. Mary's Cemetery is that over the tomb of Cavan Boa, an escaped indentured servant of George Washington's. In the burial ground at the Presbyterian Meeting House there is a tomb whose inscription begins, "Here lies a soldier hero of the Revolution, whose identity is known but to God. . . ."

Pohick Church was restored after suffering from neglect and mutilation following the Civil War, and the Presbyterian Meeting House was rebuilt after lightning set it afire. Christ Church has been more fortunate. The building is largely original, never having needed extensive restoration. Even the lettering on the beautiful tablets on either side of the pulpit, done in 1773, is believed to be original. Early Alexandrians referred to Christ Church at various times as "The Church" or "The Church nigh Alexandria" or "The Church in the woods." In Christ Church, Washington shares honors with Robert Edward Lee, the South's beloved leader, who was a member of this historic church and helped pick the Christmas greens for the Church when he was a small boy. Many Presidents of the United States come to Alexandria to worship in Christ Church during the years they live in the White House, and sit in Washington's pew during the service.

The original high-backed pews of old churches were built to cut off drafts. They also helped to keep inside each pew the little heat given by the charcoal foot-warmers that the women brought with them.

The first fire company organized in Alexandria was the Friendship Fire Company. In 1774, when Washington was attending the Continental Congress in Philadelphia, he ordered a fire engine for this company. This little hand-pumper is preserved in the Friendship Fire Company's museum in Alexandria. The company's fire mark, a metal plaque showing two clasped hands, is also on view along with early fire fighting equipment.

A fire mark on a building indicated that the owner was insured. Each insurance company had its distinctive plaque, so that the volunteer firemen would know from which company to claim their reward for putting out the fire. This system encouraged competitive fire companies and rival fire fighters to organize. At the first alarm, the firemen grabbed the heavy linen bags in which they carried valuables from the burning building, and pulling their engine and equipment over the streets, raced to the fire. The first company to reach the scene had the exclusive right to put out the fire and collect the reward. If, as sometimes happened, two companies arrived at the same time, the members of the bucket brigades sometimes engaged in a heated argument. Meanwhile, as fistfighting took precedence over fire fighting, the distraught homeowner stood by helplessly while his property was reduced to a smoking ruin.

A children's chant highlights one of the problems of the rival companies in getting to a fire:

> The SUN is in the mud,
> The STAR is in the mire,
> But the good old FRIENDSHIP
> Is putting out the fire.

111

Photo by Marler, Alexandria, Va.

The little fire engine that George Washington purchased in Philadelphia
for the citizens of Alexandria, at their request.

112

Many Alexandrians were more adept at their trade than the firemen, however. The work of the silversmiths, in particular, was outstanding. Local descendants of many Alexandria families still own beautiful pieces of silver made for their ancestors during the Revolution, and examples of the work of these artisans are collectors' items.

A little known branch of the silversmiths' art at the time was the silver ornaments used in Indian trade. Silver trinkets were very valuable as tokens of friendship and in bartering for furs. The Indians wore them as headbands, bracelets, rings, and brooches, and suspended them from their nose, ears, and neck. They put on as many as they had, all at the same time.

Ropewalks for the manufacture of cordage could be found in every American
seaport.

Combining fine workmanship with banking, silversmith were the aristocrats of the crafts.

Photo by Charles Baptie, Annandale, Va.

These extraordinarily beautiful examples of the Alexandria silversmiths' art are part of a private collection in Alexandria. Most were made when Alexandria's shipping ceased and other industries were developed.

CHAPTER ELEVEN

Seaport Without Ships

The last ball at which colonial Alexandria honored the English monarch was held in the winter of 1773-74. The man who drew the King's name out of a hat paid the cost; the women who drew the Queen's name baked the cake. The guests, dressed in finest silks, satins and laces, danced till morning. There was a break for a bountiful supper, with a wide choice of beverages, but no tea. Alexandrians sympathized with the citizens of the port of Boston. America was on the brink of war.

The account of the Boston Tea Party shocked the people of Alexandria. When the port of Boston was closed, Alexandrians subscribed to a fund to help its citizens. They sent them 273 pounds sterling, 38 barrels of flour, and 150 bushels of wheat. Washington and Mason contributed to the relief fund, which was raised at the same time that both families suffered personal losses.

117

George Mason's wife, thirty-nine years old, who had been under the care of Dr. James Craik of Alexandria, died in March 1773, after a long illness. Mason spent the eleven days following her funeral alone in his study, writing his will. Although he was only in his late 40's, he wrote as if his life was ended, too.

When Mrs. Mason died, Washington rode over to Gunston Hall and made a condolence call on his friend. A few days later, Mrs. Washington's seventeen-year-old daughter, Patsy, died. Now it was Mason's turn to go and offer sympathy.

There was another final farewell that summer. The George William Fairfaxes left Belvoir for a visit to England and never returned, ending the visits at the estate halfway between Mount Vernon and Gunston Hall.

Despite their personal concerns, Washington and Mason made frequent trips to Alexandria that summer on public business. The town, now twenty-five years old, had a population of about 2,000 people living in some 200 houses and their "dependencies," as the servants' quarters, offices, and other outbuildings were called. Community affairs, which included those of the county court and parish church, brought the town's trustees, gentlemen justices, and vestrymen to Alexandira. Mason, in particular, actively participated in all of these functions.

The annual election of members to the House of Burgesses, Virginia's Colonial legislative body, was held as usual in Alexandria's courthouse during the summer of 1774. There was no secret ballot then; voting was by voice vote. The voter gave his name and announced the candidate he voted for, and the election clerks wrote this down. Washington was one of the candidates, and was elected. His supporters gathered around the hogshead of toddy in the Market Square and drank to his health. As was customary, Washington gave a ball that evening and his account book carefully lists the cost of the cake, ale and fiddler. Coffee and chocolate were served, but the Alexandria women loyally supported their Boston sisters and again did not drink tea.

Alexandria was alarmed by the British government's strict enforcement of her revenue policy after the French and Indian war. Great Britain's economic measures of direct or indirect taxation stirred up resentment in Alexandria as they did in the other cities and towns. The colonists considered these acts of a Parliament in which they had no representation as infringing on their rights and sought protection of the liberties to which they felt that they were entitled as Englishmen.

All during that summer meetings were called throughout the colonies to discuss the serious political aspects of the Boston Port Bill. On the day before the Fairfax County meeting was scheduled to be held in Alexandria, Mason met Washington at church and went with him to Mount Vernon for a conference, as Washington was chairman of the meeting. They talked so late that Mason spent the night at Mount Vernon and the next day the two men rode up to Alexandria together to attend the meeting.

Unfortunately, there is no eye-witness account of the historic scene in the Fairfax County courthouse in Alexandria on July 18, 1774. Washington, as presiding officer, read the twenty-four resolutions prepared by Mason that are known as the Fairfax Resolves. In these, Mason set forth the rights and grievances of the colonists. Two sentences read: "We came equals into this world, and equals shall we go out of it. All men are by nature born equally free and independent." In the Declaration of Independence two years later, Thomas

Jefferson rephrased and streamlined this idea to read: "All men are created equal."

The Alexandrians and their neighbors were British subjects, and the Fairfax Resolves did not advocate a definite break with the mother country. That such a break was an acknowledged possibility though, is evident in the equipment listed for the militia organized six months later.

Standing around the Market Square, Alexandrians watched Washington's initial preparations as military leader of the rebellious American colonies. He came to town often that summer to meet and review the volunteer companies. There were two of these companies formed in Alexandria at the beginning of the Revolution, about 150 men in all. One group was made up of "gentlemen" and the other of "mechanics." The latter wore red and blue uniforms. The former, the Fairfax Independent Company, wore a uniform of blue, turned up with buff, with plain yellow metal buttons, a buff waistcoat and breeches, and white stockings. This was the uniform that Washington wore.

There were opportunities for Mason to test his abilities in Alexandria, too. On one occasion, when the courthouse badly needed repairing, the usual method of paying for the work, by a court ordered tobacco levy, was proposed. Mason objected. He argued that the newly adopted Virginia Constitution, containing the Declaration of Rights, which he wrote, expressly prohibited this method of taxation as unconstitutional. He pointed out that the power to tax was held by the elected representatives of the people, the Virginia Assembly. This was a new viewpoint on taxing to his listeners. Mason finally convinced them, but the vote was close.

It is said that Mason could explain the most complicated ideas in an understandable way, whether verbally or in writing, but he participated in public affairs reluctantly. He was impatient with work that had to be done in committees. He was a chronic gout sufferer and was in pain a good deal of time. And, lastly, he wanted to stay close to Gunston Hall to look after his motherless children.

The oldest of the nine orphans was twenty, and the youngest three years old. When William Ramsay, in behalf of Alexandria's voters, asked Mason after Washington left to become Commander-in-Chief to fill Washington's vacant position in the Virginia legislature, Mason gave as his excuse that he had to look after his children. (He finally relented and did become a member of the Virginia Assembly.) At another time, in Richmond, when Patrick Henry and Thomas Jefferson backed by two-thirds of the members in convention insisted that Mason represent Virginia in the Philadelphia Congress, he stood before his colleagues and pled for the right to refuse. The clerk recorded that he spoke so eloquently in his children's behalf that tears ran down the cheeks of the presiding officer.

Washington spent almost nine years during the Revolutionary War away from Mount Vernon but his family worries followed him to battlefield headquarters. Mrs. Washington had so spoiled her only surviving child, John Parke Custis, that Washington had a hard time trying to help the boy. Young Custis left school, married, and began buying property from the Alexander family, including some back of where the National Airport now is. His stepson agreed to such excessively costly financial arrangements for the house and land that it shocked Washington. He wrote long letters of disapproval and advice, which Custis ignored.

The newlywed Custis couple moved into Abingdon, the former home of Gerard Alexander, one of the

General Washington reviewing his troops. Scenes such as this were repeated many times during the Revolutionary War. Washington's first and last troop review took place on the Market Square in Alexandria.

original trustees of Alexandria. Three little girls were born to Custis and his wife in rapid succession. Six months after a son arrived, the father joined Washington in the field, where he contracted camp fever and died. Later, the Washingtons took the two youngest children, Eleanor and George Washington Parke Custis, to Mount Vernon. Much later, Eleanor Custis and her husband, Lawrence Lewis, built Woodlawn, about two miles south of Mount Vernon, on land that Washington had given them; her brother built the house now known as the Custis-Lee Mansion on part of the property he had inherited from his father, where Arlington National Cemetery is today.

During the Revolution Washington was encamped far from Alexandria but he knew that many of the mer-

122

chants there were critical of him and opposed to the war with Great Britain. They had lost their biggest flour customer and all other shipping had come to a virtual standstill. Opposition to the war came from others in Alexandria, notably the Quakers. There were a great number of them in the town and they flatly refused to contribute to the war because of religious principles. War work went on among the other residents, however. The women, especially, were busy raising money, first for arms and then for widows and orphans. Carlyle lost his only son, a boy of seventeen.

During the war, a severe epidemic of smallpox quarantined the whole town. The townspeople and a regiment of soldiers quartered in Alexandria were inoculated against the dread disease. Hundreds of slaves were vaccinated on the plantations. Many people died and Dr. William Richman, director of the hospital in Alexandria, was suspended for the fatal results of his inoculations. Later, he was exonerated by the Medical Committee of the Continental Congress. Nicholas Cresswell, who had come to Alexandria, from England, to seek his fortune, graphically described the situation: "Such a pock-eyed place I never was in before."

The people suffered when they could not longer buy essential imported products. Salt, an absolute necessity in preserving pork and fish, the principal foods in the daily diet, was soon in short supply. Washington's manager at Mount Vernon reported to him that the people in the Alexandria vicinity were desperately in need of salt. When a sloop arrived in Alexandria one day with a load of salt, men from the back country tried to unload it by force to make sure that they got some of the scarce preservative, and Alexandrians stayed behind locked doors in fear of violence.

On the lighter side of the war, there were occasional glimpses of military leaders passing through the town. The Marquis de Lafayette visited Alexandria for the first time in 1777. The Baron Johann de Kalb was with him. A story still heard in Alexandria is that the Frenchman, the German, and their host at the City Tavern, John Dalton, were in the dead center of a language impasse when John Paul Jones fortunately arrived and took over as interpreter. After the surrender of Lord Cornwallis at Yorktown, the forces of Comte de Rochambeau, General of the French Army during the Revolutionary War, encamped north of Alexandria. There is an exquisite watercolor of the town among a series of original drawings made by the French engineers of the various camps and their surroundings. The bridge which now connects Washington and Virginia a few miles to the north of the French encampment is called the Rochambeau Bridge.

A newcomer to Alexandria was Nicholas Cresswell, a young Englishman whose hopes of quickly making a fortune in America were ruined by the Revolution. He was advised to go into the business of trading with the Indians. This, it was pointed out, would at the same time take him away from Alexandria where he was liable to arrest as an enemy. Before going west into Indian territory, Cresswell ordered a variety of trinkets from an Alexandria silversmith. He hung these all over himself, covering his calico shirt with silver brooches and his arms with silver armplates. He hoped this disguise would fool any unfriendly Indians. Luckily, the first Indians he met were friendly, because a first glance showed him how unlike them he looked. True, they dressed in some of the white man's clothing, although the Indians wore loin cloths in place of trousers. As for the silver orna-

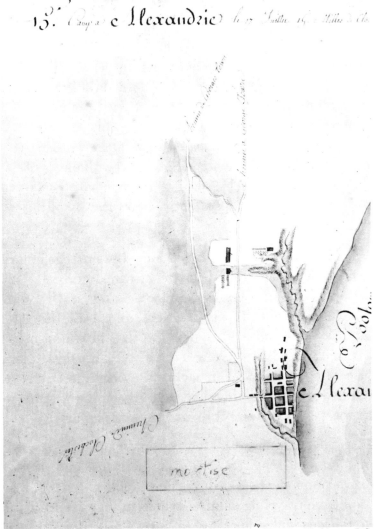

An old watercolor shows the Comte de Rochambeau's army, returning to France, passed through Alexandria in 1782 and pitched camp on the outskirts of the town. They then crossed the Potomac River to Georgetown.

125

ments, Cresswell knew that he could never imitate the way they wore these:

> They have rings of silver in their nose and bobs to them which hang over their upper lip. Their ears are cut from the tips two thirds of the way round and the piece extended with brass wire till it touches their shoulders. In this part they hang a thick silver plate, wrought in flourishes of about three inches in diameter, with plates of silver round their arms and in their hair, which is all cut off except a long lock on the top of the head.

Two of the ornaments which Indians customarily wore suspended around the neck, called gorgets, and a skippet, the little box which protects the seal that was used to ratify the Treaty of Ghent, all made by an Alexandria silversmith, are now in the Museum of the American Indian in New York City. The silver trowel used by Washington in laying the cornerstone for the United States Capitol and the silver spurs worn by Robert E. Lee were also made in Alexandria.

Silversmiths also doubled as clock- and watch-makers and repairers, jewelers, opticians, and even on occasion as dentists. But resident dentists had competition from traveling dentists, who sent an advance notice to the local newspaper and set up a temporary office and laboratory in the center of town. They also visited the plantations. Washington, late in life, had false teeth but the myth that he had some teeth made of wood ignores the obvious danger from splinters.

The same dentist who attended the Mount Vernon family placed the following notice in the Alexandria newspaper:

> Dr. LeMoyeur, Dentist, lately from New York,
> who transplants teeth, will be in Alexandria in
> a few days where he will stay for a short time.
> Inquire for him at the Printing Office.

He apparently did a rushing business in teeth transplanting and soon ran out of material, and placed another advertisement in the paper:

> Any person wishing to part with their foreteeth, may hear of a purchaser by calling at
> Mr. Perrin's Store.

In the final months of the Revolutionary War there was a naval engagement on the Potomac River south of Alexandria. The *Ranger,* an armed brigantine with a crew of twenty, sailed down the river and met two enemy craft with thirty men each. They engaged in a desperate battle during which the enemy counted all but ten of its men killed or wounded. The *Ranger,* with one dead and several wounded, returned to Alexandria.

One day in October, 1781, the voice of the town crier resounded in the streets of Alexandria. A dancing and cheering crowd followed him. As he came by, people rushed to their doors to hear the news: "Cornwallis is taken! Cornwallis is taken!"

At the war's end, the inherent weakness of the national government under the Articles of Confederation, that it consisted of a league of states and not a united nation, soon became evident. Problems arose that caused the states to disagree among themselves. In an effort to settle one such dispute between Virginia and Maryland, a meeting was called in Alexandria in the spring of 1785 to discuss the regulation and control of navigation on the Potomac River. When the Maryland delegation arrived on the date set for the meeting, they

The town crier calls out the news of the British defeat at Yorktown, Va. The victory, accomplished by the American and French forces, ended the Revolutionary War.

found that the Virginians had not been notified. Washington invited the disappointed men to Mount Vernon and sent word to Gunston Hall asking Mason, one member of the Virginia delegation, to join them there. The discussions continued for more than a week. In history this meeting, known as the Mount Vernon Convention, is important because it emphasized what good might be accomplished if representatives from all the states could meet and discuss matters of mutual

128

interest. The ultimate in such "a meeting of the minds" was the Constitutional Convention in Philadelphia and the framing of the new government.

Alexandrians anxiously awaited news of the action taken by the individual states on ratifying the Constitution. Finally, the message came from their capital: Virginia had voted in favor of ratification. Joyfully, the people made arrangements to celebrate. Just before dawn on the day set, word was received that the number of states necessary to put the Constitution into effect had ratified the document. The elated Washington wrote from Mount Vernon on June 28, 1788:

> Thus the Citizens of Alexandria, when convened, constituted the first public company in America, which had the pleasure of pouring libation to the prosperity of . . . the general government.

An early view of the White House. Umbrellas, or parasols, were greatly in vogue, even by those on horseback.

130

CHAPTER TWELVE

The Establishment of a National Capital

The beginning of the United States as an independent nation ushered in a period of unprecedented prosperity for Alexandria. This upsurge in business was the direct cause of the town's phenomenally rapid growth. In a single decade Alexandria's population almost doubled, numbering about 5,000 people who lived in some 800 buildings, exclusive of servants' quarters. Beautiful houses, elegantly furnished, formed a perfect setting for the wealthy merchant princes and their families. In the very last year of the eighteenth century, Alexandria celebrated its golden anniversary.

Of course, when George Washington was unanimously chosen as first president of the new Republic, there was special rejoicing in Alexandria, where he was thought of as a native son. An immediate problem facing him was to select the site for the national capital. States-

131

The beginning of the United States as an independent nation also marked a period of great prosperity for Alexandria. Beautifully furnished homes provided the perfect settings for wealthy Alexandria merchants. The second-floor parlor of the house at 200 Prince St., Alexandria (now the Alexandria Room in the City Art Museum of St. Louis, Mo.) shows the gracious style of living at the time.

men from the various sections of the country wanted the capital city within, or adjacent to, their respective localities. Virginia's delegate to the Continental Congress,

Henry Lee, Jr., Robert E. Lee's grandfather, introduced the resolution for a site on the Potomac.

Thomas Jefferson had urged for a resolution to hold a session of Congress at Alexandria, but failed. His name recurs frequently in connection with Alexandria at this time. He had high hopes for the town's future and wrote in a letter from Paris: "Alexandria on the Potomac will undoubtedly become a very great place." When he disembarked at Alexandria on his return from his post as Minister to France in 1790, the mayor welcomed him formally. It was then, according to tradition, that Jefferson suggested the hilltop where the George Washington Masonic National Memorial was later built as the site for the Capitol of the United States.

The permanent location for the nation's capital was finally reached through a compromise, and the site, ten square miles, included all of Alexandria. In July 1790, Congress passed a law known as the Residence Act setting certain boundary limitations along the Potomac but giving the President the final choice of the exact area to be occupied by the Federal district, stipulated as not exceeding ten miles square. The following January, President Washington by proclamation directed that the location of the first corner of the Federal district be determined by running experimental lines from the courthouse in Alexandria to Hunting Creek, the town's southern boundary. And Congress, in the final hours of that session amended the Residence Act in accordance with the President's proclamation: the limit of the Federal territory was extended and the town of Alexandria was included in the ten miles square. The amendatory act reaffirmed a stipulation that was part of the original act. This proviso reads: "Provided, that nothing herein contained shall authorize the erection of the public buildings otherwise than on the Maryland side of the River Potomac, as required by the aforesaid act."

Most Alexandrians were probably unaware of the Congressional curb. In any event, it did not affect their enthusiasm. In 1779, Alexandria's form of government had been changed, giving the citizens a voice in it. Under the charter of the Act of Incorporation, an elected twelve member Common Council replaced the twelve trustees of the first form of government. The Common Council selected from among themselves the Mayor, Recorder and four Aldermen; the rest were the Common Councilmen. The latter had no share in judicial functions but all twelve sat for legislative business. They adopted the design of the common seal, a ship in full sail with a balance poised about it, indicating trade and just dealing. Alexandrians anticipated great benefits under their new local government, and expected an added beneficial advantage from being included in the new Federal district. When the official Geographer General, Andrew Ellicott, arrived they met him with a warm welcome.

Ellicott followed President Washington's instructions for determining the exact location of the first corner of the ten mile square. He began at the southwest corner of Fairfax and Cameron Streets. He set up a Surveyor's Camp on the outskirts of the town as he planned to spend most of the summer working in the Alexandria vicinity.

As soon as Ellicott had drawn his experimental lines and set the exact spot on Alexandria's southern boundary from which to start the survey, President Washington issued his second proclamation designating Jones Point as the point of beginning of the Federal City. On April 15, 1791, the cornerstone was placed there with appropriate ceremonies. Washington was making a tour of the Southern states and could not attend, but the Masonic Lodge of Alexandria, of which he was a member, participated.

Historic Jones Point, the beginning point of Mistress Margaret Brent's grant in 1654, now served once again as an important cornerstone. Because of Washington's proclamation of 1791, people throughout the nation heard of the Point.

A remarkable number of events and activities have taken place on this relatively tiny spot of land where George Jones opened a tavern in 1818. During a yellow fever epidemic when one in ten of Alexandria's citizens died, a hospital isolation center was located at Jones Point. Fortifications and shipyards were built on the little cape several times. A beacon, the oldest inland lighthouse in the United States, is directly over the cornerstone, and has guided ships past here since 1855. The Woodrow Wilson Bridge crosses the Potomac at Jones Point. A fifty-acre national park, to include the lighthouse and cornerstone, is in the planning stage.

The John A. Washington Family by John Gadsby Chapman. This painting is in the George Washington Masonic National Memorial in Alexandria. John A. Washington, Jr., who appears here as a child, was the last of the Washington family to live at Mount Vernon.

CHAPTER THIRTEEN

Life at the Close of the Century

Alexandria, as a part of the national capital, hoped for increased economic benefits at home and abroad, since her trade was no longer confined to England and the difficulties with France and Spain had been settled. There was still one unresolved serious drawback to commerce and trade on a worldwide scale. Pirates continued their raids on American ships. George Mason's son, John, en route to open a branch business office in France, sent a message back to his partner in Georgetown, on the outskirts of the Federal city, by pilot boat requesting insurance coverage in the amount of six or seven hundred pounds in case he should be captured by pirates. One Alexandria man who did go through this experience but was later released was Captain James McKenzie, master of a ship sailing from Alexandria on a regular schedule.

Alexandria was, of course, the home port of many seafaring men. Their families lived in the town, in the houses their men built for them overlooking the river, where they anxiously watched and waited for them to come back. Some never did. It is said that one captain's widow still haunts Red Hill, a high point with a view of the Alexandria harbor. A newcomer in the neighborhood looked out of her window one summer evening and saw a tall, slender young woman, her long cloak billowing in the breeze, standing motionless in the garden, gazing toward the river. In answer to her "Hello! Won't you come in?" the apparition vanished. Alexandrians say that the ghost of Red Hill has often been seen.

Captain McKenzie was typical of the colorful and daring seamen who profited from Alexandria's prosperity. A few years after his arrival from Scotland he was master of his own ship. One morning in 1798 the *Lexington*, loaded with tobacco bound for Holland, lay in the harbor at Alexandria waiting for the captain and his bride-to-be to come on board. The couple arrived with a minister from Maryland and the marriage ceremony was performed in full view of the British man-of-war anchored nearby. Then the *Lexington* sailed down the Potomac taking Captain and Mrs. McKenzie on their wedding trip.

That the clergyman was from Maryland stresses the unusual boundary between that state and Virginia. The Potomac River, to the shores of "the Kingdom of Virginia," is part of the original grant made by King Charles I in 1632 to Lord Baltimore. In 1776, Virginia acknowledged Maryland's right to the Potomac River.

We do not know in exactly which Alexandria house Captain and Mrs. McKenzie lived when they returned from their honeymoon, but it might have been one of those lining both sides of the cobblestone street called

Sea Captains' Row. According to tradition, the cobblestones paving this first block of Prince Street were brought over as ballast on ships, and are said to have been laid by Hessian mercenaries during the Revolutionary War. The houses are crowded close together, their front doors opening directly onto the street, their rooftops resembling giant steps leading from the river up the steep hill. Each house has a pocket handkerchief size garden in the rear. This street, more than any other in Alexandria, retains its early appearance.

The McKenzie's son, Lewis, lived in the George William Fairfax House on the second block of Prince Street. He is said to have installed the first bathtub with running water in Alexandria. The drain from the tub passed through a hole in the wall, splashing the water down on the garden three floors below.

Some second generation Alexandrians moved to much larger and more elegant houses than their parents had occupied. Alexandria's merchants and others engaged in trade had grown very prosperous. Although a merchant usually still used the first floor of his house for his business, the double connecting drawing rooms in the family living quarters above were known as the ballroom.

The new houses built during the 1790's were in the formal Georgian style. The gracious atmosphere that prevailed behind their lovely fanlighted doorways with shining brass knockers was created mainly by the imported luxury items of their furnishings. Windows were hung with wooden Venetian blinds and rich fabrics; walls with handsomely framed mirrors that reflected ancestral portraits. Dinner tables were covered with fine linen and laid with delicate china, glass, and handwrought silver. Shining fireplace equipment and beautiful mahogany furniture gleamed in the light of the

An early view of Sea Captains' Row, the 100 block of Prince Street. According to tradition, the cobblestones in this street were laid by Hessian mercenaries.

The 100 block of Prince Street today.

The new houses built in Alexandria in the 1790's were in formal Georgian style. This ballroom is from Gadsby's Tavern, now in the American Wing of the Metropolitan Museum of Art in New York City. (This famous room has also been reconstructed in Gadsby's Tavern, Alexandria.)

beeswax candles in crystal chandeliers high above the carpeted floors.

Amazing growth had taken place during the life-times of the founders and their plantation neighbors. In 1754, Ramsay made an entry in his ledger that Major George Washington had received two pounds, three shillings, and four pence. In 1791, Secretary of the Treasury, Alexander Hamilton, instructed Charles Lee, Alexandria's first collector of customs, to keep a thousand dollars on hand in case the President of the United States, General Washington, needed some money.

There was no Virginia bank in 1791. The nearest one to Alexandria was in Baltimore. When John Mason returned from France bringing with him a large amount of gold, and stopped over in Richmond, Mason wrote to his son cautioning him to put the money in the state treasurer's iron chest for safekeeping.

The Bank of Alexandria was chartered in 1792. Washington was a stockholder and depositor. He later bequeathed twenty shares of the bank stock toward the support of a free school connected with the Alexandria Academy. When the bank first opened, William Herbert, Carlyle's son-in-law, put the day's receipts in the Carlyle house every night. The first bank building was on the corner of Carlyle's property, at Fairfax and Cameron Streets. It still exists today incorporated in that corner of the Carlyle Apartments.

The same year that the bank was chartered, the Apothecary Shop was built a little over a block away, at 107 South Fairfax Street. Two bay windows displaying graceful apothecary jars filled with brightly colored water flank the double entrance doors. Gold labels gleam on the bottles that fill the shelves, row upon row. Mortars and pestles of various sizes, scales, and wooden medicine chests, with compartments for leeches, are on

143

The Bank of Alexandria where George Washington kept his money. A fire-proof, shallow closet served as the bank vault. The original vault is still said to exist, but is hidden behind the wall panelling of the building now on the bank's site.

144

The Bank of Alexandria was chartered in 1792. The first bank building was erected on the corner of John Carlyle's property, at Fairfax and Cameron, and still stands today in a corner of the Carlyle Apartments.

145

display on the counters above the mahogany drawers. The dark amber, green, or cobalt blue prescription bottles are in color for practical reasons. The dark glass protected the contents from light deterioration and warned those who could not read that the medicine might be poisonous. The bottles containing poisons also had a rough finish as an added precaution.

The Stabler-Leadbeater Apothecary Shop is now a museum, owned and maintained by the Landmarks Society, which was organized in 1933 when the drug store closed. It was in continuous business for almost one hundred and fifty years, owned and operated by the same family during all that time. The shop's pharmaceutical collection is considered one of the finest of its kind, but the special interest in the museum lies in its historic associations. Washington, Mason, Lee and almost everybody else in old Alexandria bought drugs and picked up their mail there. In the musty old files is a note from Martha Washington: "Mrs. Washington desires Mr. Stabler to send by bearer a quart bottle of his best castor oil and a bill for it."

The founder of the Apothecary Shop, Edward Stabler, served as first librarian for the subscription library founded by the Alexandria Library Company in 1794. The books were probably kept in a room back of the pharmacy. Subscribers paid five dollars as an initial fee and then four dollars annually. Non-members could "hire" books at nominal rates. Library finances once reached a low of seven cents in the treasury but the library survived and was incorporated in 1799. It continued as a private institution until 1937, when the Library Company gave its book collection and equipped a building on Queen Street. This is part of the public library building, greatly expanded. It has no basement, in accordance with a stipulation in the ninety-nine-year

The Stabler-Leadbeater Apothecary Shop, where George Washington purchased all his drugs and picked up his mail, is now a museum. It was in continuous business for almost 150 years. The shop's pharmaceutical collection is considered one of the finest of its kind.

lease from the Quakers, who originally used the site as a burial ground. The Alexandria Library Company still exists, limited to forty members elected for life, and has revived its traditional annual lecture meeting.

The Alexandria Library offers its borrowers thousands of books and hundreds of films. It has added two branch libraries to the original one. Its outstanding collection of books and other material on state and local history is especially noteworthy, and in the Virginia Room, a reader can find the answer to a single question

147

Detail of the interior of the Stabler-Leadbeater Apothecary Shop at 107 South Fairfax Street, Alexandria.

on history or do extensive research. Among the many old and rare books in the Alexandria Library is "A Medical Dictionary" published in London in 1743, given by

George Washington in Alexandria. After attending to business at his bank, he had only a short walk to the Stabler-Leadbeater Apothecary Shop for his mail.

George Washington to his physician, Dr. James Craik, and later presented to the Library Company.

Many other local physicians achieved fame. Washington appointed Dr. William Brown to the post of Physician-General and Director of Hospitals of the Continental Army. Dr. Elisha Cullen Dick is remembered in history as one of the physicians who attended Washington in his last illness. Dr. Dick was Alexandria's quarantine officer and built the hospital at Jones Point during the yellow fever epidemic. Dr. Dick, two

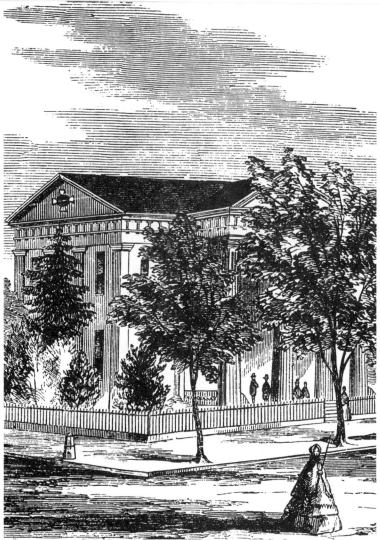

The Alexandria Library Company was begun in a room back of the Stabler-Leadbeater Apothecary Shop, with Edward Stabler serving as its first librarian. Later the library was housed in the Alexandria Lyceum (above). The Company continued as a private institution until 1937, when it gave its book collection to the building on Queen St.

members of his family, and a young student living in his house all caught the dread disease, which was brought into Alexandria by a ship's crew.

150

Dr. Dick enjoyed writing verses and an invitation to one dinner at his house reads:

> If you can eat a good fat duck,
> Come up with us and take pot luck.
> Of white-backs we have got a pair,
> So plump, so round, so fat, so fair,
> An London alderman would fight,
> Through pies and tarts, to get one bite.
> Moreover we have beef or pork,
> That you may use your knife and fork.
> Come up precisely at two o'clock,
> The door shall open at your knock.
> The day 'tho wet, the streets 'tho muddy,
> To keep out the cold, we'll have some toddy.
> And if perchance you should get sick,
> You'll have at hand, Yours, E. C. Dick.

The flag of the *Alexandria Gazette*. The design pictures the first printing press and the motif "The pen is mightier than the sword."

CHAPTER FOURTEEN

Eighteenth Century News

T he medical ethics of the day permitted advertising. Alexandria's doctors advertised medicines for sale and used the columns of the local newspaper to fight a price war for the available "snake-root and bees-wax." They also fought competition from abroad. A European doctor placed a notice in the Alexandria newspaper stating that he cured King's evil, falling sickness, dropsies, smallpox, and consumption; also, deafness and cancer, if curable. He informed the readers that he planned to give lectures, or private instruction if preferred, on midwifery.

The *Alexandria Gazette,* still published, proudly boasts that it is the oldest newspaper in continuous circulation in America. Its first issue, printed on February 5, 1784, proclaimed that inasmuch as America was now a political entity, ranking as sovereign and independent among the nations of the world, a weekly newspaper was to be published in Alexandria. Its title at that time was

The Virginia Journal & Alexandria Advertiser. Later published twice a week, the *Alexandria Gazette* is now a daily.

Very little local news was included when the paper was first published. Advertisements, notices of the arrival and departure of ships, with lists of the merchandise they carried, took precedence in the newspaper columns of the seaport town. If a local event was important enough, it was mentioned, "The Marquis de la Fayette accompanied by . . . the Captain of the Dragoons in the Army of France, passed thru this town on his way to his Excellency, General Washington's Seat, Mount Vernon."

Notices of runaway wives, and of slaves, appeared on the front page, as did all advertising. Tobacco, corn, wheat, flour and ships' bread were offered for sale. Fish in season were listed as acceptable in exchange for other commodities. Stage and mail schedules were prominently printed. The three-day journey from New York to Alexandria, with stopovers in Philadelphia and Baltimore, once cost four dollars per day. The post rider arrived weekly.

Private schools and instructors listed their specialties in the newspaper. Frenchmen, recently soldiers in the army, announced the start of classes in their language. A school where young ladies were taught needlework and writing opened. A music master offered instruction on the harpsichord, violin, German flute, and the guitar. A six months' subscription to concerts on every Saturday evening followed by a ball was advertised for twenty dollars the season.

Some of Alexandria's young women were members of social clubs, but a rigidly observed custom of the times deemed it highly improper for a woman's name to appear in the public press except at her birth, marriage, or death. In order to publicize an important matter through the local newspaper, the following notice was placed:

At a full meeting of the Ladies (who dance at the Alexandria Assemblies) held last night at the house of Mrs. Ceremony, on motion of Miss Prudentia, seconded by Miss Lovely, the following resolutions were agreed to:

1st. Resolved, that no Lady accept of a partner at the next Assembly, who has not supplied himself with either white kid or white silk gloves.

An amendment was proposed by Miss Evergreen (of great experience) that Buckskin or coloured gloves should be admitted but this motion fell on its not being seconded.

2d. Resolved, that the above resolution be published in the *Columbia Mirror and Times,* that timely notice may be given to the gloveless gentry.

Lucy Tulip, S.P.T.

February 7th.

Washington chose a court day, when crowds would gather in the town, to place an advertisement offering 30,000 acres of his western land for lease. Mason thought that a good time to advertise for a carpenter to build a house. He assured the applicant that payments would be punctual.

In the November 8, 1792 issue of the paper, the following obituary appeared:

On the 14th Ult., died, at Gunston Hall, in this County, the Hon. George Mason, Esquire. In addition to his eminent talents as a Statesmen, he was a Gentleman of Great Virtue and Patriotism.

On December 16, 1799, the Alexandria newspaper informed its readers:

> It is our painful duty first to announce to our Country and to the world, the death of their illustrious benefactor—
>
> ### GEORGE WASHINGTON
>
> This mournful event occurred on Saturday evening, about 11 o'clock. On the preceding night, he was attacked with a violent inflammatory affection of the throat, which in less than four and twenty hours put a period to his mortal existence. Conscious of his approaching dissolution, he bore the excruciating agonies of a violent and painful disease with that heroic and Christian fortitude for which he was ever distinguished, and expired in the possession of that serenity of mind resulting from a consciousness of integrity, and a well-spent life.

CHAPTER FIFTEEN

Alexandria, D.C.: 1791-1847

W hen the Federal government and its entire personnel of 132 employees moved from Philadelphia to Washington in June, 1800, only two public buildings in the capital were even partially completed, the Senate wing of the Capitol and the White House. It would have been possible to house the whole government force of that day in the White House when finished, give each worker a separate room, and have the East Room available for group gatherings.

Land speculators had bought blocks of the woodland and swamps staked out by surveyors in the mosquito-infested wilderness which, except for some farms and Georgetown, was the area set aside for the capital on the east bank of the Potomac River. Builders had hurriedly put up clumps of houses, willy-nilly. Rough trails connected them. A horse might sink knee-deep in mud, or raise a cloud of dust that choked and hid its

157

rider. The government temporarily set up various department offices in these buildings. There were very few private houses and the members of Congress and the Supreme Court lived as bachelors in the boarding houses that sprang up around Capitol Hill. Though the sprawling streets seemed haphazard at first, the city, as it grew, revealed the broad, tree-lined avenues and open parks plan of Pierre Charles L'Enfant. "A city of magnificent distances" is how one foreign diplomat described Washington in 1800.

In contrast Alexandria, that part of the Federal city on the west bank of the Potomac River, was a well established town. It had outgrown its original boundaries several times. Hundreds of carts, wagons and carriages clattered along the town's streets, many of which were paved with cobblestones. A wooden license plate, selling for thirty-five cents, dangled from each vehicle. It was inscribed with the letters "A C" for Alexandria Corporation. Bricklaid sidewalks had lamp posts at the corners and the night watchman who lit the lamps also called out the hours. There were several banks, tobacco warehouses, bread and biscuit bakeries, and a brewery. Merchants and shopkeepers made up Alexandria's largest single class of businessmen except for tavern keepers. There were thirty-four licensed inns in Alexandria in 1800.

The large number of taverns was necessary for the convenience of travelers because the main travel routes from near and far passed through Alexandria. When Mrs. John Adams went to call on Mrs. Washington, her trip from the White House to Mount Vernon necessitated an overnight stop in Alexandria. Travelers from abroad, disembarking at the Alexandria wharf, wrote glowing accounts of the excellent accommodations and good food they enjoyed in the town. Gadsby's, many

158

maintained, was the best in the United States, even superior to any inn in New York.

The foreign visitors must have thought some of the local customs very peculiar. They were probably fascinated, and amused, at seeing both men and women, whether on foot or on horseback, carrying open umbrellas in all seasons. They learned that the umbrellas were a protection from the sun in summer, the rain or snow in winter, and the evening dews in spring and autumn.

Another custom on which visitors commented was that at dinners and parties the women sat together, separately from the men. The men talked politics almost exclusively, a topic about which the women knew nothing, so they preferred to sit together and talk about servants and children among themselves. One familiar custom was greatly enjoyed by all the men. The barber arrived on horseback "to perform the operation of shaving," and as he did in Europe, brought the news and scandal.

Leaving Alexandria, a traveler either had to follow a waterway until he could ford it, or cross it by ferry. Before bridges were built between Alexandria and Washington, ferries crossed the Potomac River at this point. The first ferries used for public transportation were simply crude scows propelled by oars or pulled along a cable. A man paid for himself and extra for his horse. The ferry at the island just above where the Lincoln Memorial now is was an elaborate, decked affair, big enough to take on two loaded wagons. Horses stationed on the shore at each end provided the power. The island and the ferry were owned by George Mason and later, by his son, General John Mason. Official and unofficial Washington came to Alexandria via Georgetown and Mason's Ferry. Since there was no theatre in Washington until 1800, the Washingtonians often came to enjoy a fine dinner at Gadsby's and stayed on to attend a performance at Liberty Hall in the evening.

River transportation between Alexandria and Washington reached its peak in the steam power era. At first, there was keen competition between sailboats and steamboats. The sloop *Dart* made a daily round trip, charging a fare each way. The proprietor of the steamboat *Camden* assured the public in a newspaper advertisement that there was no reason for passengers to be afraid of bursting boilers. Admittedly, they frequently burst, but nothing serious happened; there was just a little delay, he explained.

As the use of steamboats increased, they were incorporated into the stage coach routes. This cut travel time drastically. Before using the steamboat for part of his journey, a passenger on the mail coach traveling to Fredericksburg, Virginia, had to leave Alexandria long before breakfast in order to arrive at his destination fifty miles away that night, having spent sixteen hours en route. After a steamboat company was organized in Alexandria in 1812, passengers made the trip in half the time.

View of Washington Street, Alexandria, looking south, circa 1850. The cotton factory in the center foreground is now an apartment house.

View of Alexandria harbor. The ship in the foreground is typical of those that crowded the busy port.

CHAPTER SIXTEEN

After the War of 1812

O n August 27, 1814, three days after they burned the White House and the Capitol, the British anchored at the Alexandria wharf and forced the citizens of the town to hand over huge supplies of flour, tobacco, cotton, and wine to them. They loaded these supplies on ships in the harbor, and sinking or burning those they did not use, sailed off with their booty. But they had spared the town.

Two years later, another English ship brought mystery, romance and an enduring legend to Alexandria. One day, a well-dressed couple walked slowly up the hill from the landing, the man solicitously supporting an obviously sick young woman. They registered at the City Hotel and asked that a doctor be called. After examining the patient, he sent for two women to take turns as nurses. Everyone in town soon knew that there was a critically ill young woman at the City Hotel. But as if

163

sworn to secrecy, neither the doctor nor his assistants would say what the young woman was suffering from, or even what her name was.

Stories concerning the mysterious young woman circulated around town. One that has survived is that she had been the ward of an elderly lord and had refused to marry him. In a heated argument between her guardian and a young suitor, his lordship fell to the floor, striking his head on the stone, and died. The young couple had taken the first ship for America.

Several weeks later, in spite of all that the doctor and his volunteer nurses could do, their patient died. The young man ordered a tombstone for her grave, but gave no name in the inscription carved in the stone. He explained that this was what the dead woman had wanted. She had come to Alexandria as a stranger, and she wished to be remembered as a stranger forever. Numerous efforts have been made to find out who she was but all that is actually known of the Female Stranger is carved in stone over her grave in St. Paul's Cemetery:

To the Memory of a
FEMALE STRANGER
whose mortal sufferings terminated
on the 14th day of October 1816
Aged 23 years and 8 months
This stone is placed by her disconsolate
husband in whose arms she sighed out her
last breath and who under God
did his utmost even to soothe the cold
ear of death.
How loved, how valued once avails thee not,
To whom related, or by whom begot.

A heap of dust alone remains of thee
'Tis all thou art and all the proud shall be.
To Him gave all the Prophets witness that
through His name whosoever believeth in Him
shall receive remission of sins.

Acts: 10th Chapter 43rd verse.

At about this time, during the first quarter of the
nineteenth century, many Alexandria businessmen became interested in a new venture. Canals, which would
open up the Western lands, had a special appeal to those
who owned land in Kentucky. A company was formed
and many invested heavily in building waterways into
the interior. The first canals were completed in 1829 but
railroads, the newest in transportation, made them obsolete even before they were used.

It was at this time, too, that a disastrous fire burned
out the heart of the business section of Alexandria. The
great fire of 1827 broke out at nine o'clock the morning
of January 18th, in thirteen-degree weather, starting on
the east side of Royal Street between King and Prince
Streets. Two hours later, the first engines finally arrived
from Capitol Hill to help the local volunteer company.
The Washington Bridge Company threw open the gates
of the Potomac River bridge and charged no tolls for the
people of Georgetown, Washington, and the 300 men
from the Navy Yard who rushed to help man the pumps
in the burning town. The Union Stage line dispatched its
huge steamboat stage down the Potomac, with the
United States hose wagon on board and a score of men to
pull it to the fire from the landing.

As the water poured from the hoses, it froze, covering the firemen with coats of ice. One fire engine froze.
Every man, woman and child joined the bucket brigades
formed at the river's edge, and for five hours passed con-

tainers that they had hurriedly snatched up from hand to hand. Forty to fifty houses—the count varied, depending on whether or not certain "dependencies" were included—valued at more than $100,000 were destroyed.

The import-export business houses were particularly hard-hit by the fire. Fish, after wheat, was Alexandria's leading export in the early 1800's. Washington, in his diary, had commented on the well-stocked Potomac River, with the various kinds of fish according to the season. He listed the abundance of shad, sturgeon, herrings, and perch. Jefferson, in his plantation book, noted that a barrel of fish went as far with his farm laborers as 200 pounds of pork. In 1812, he complained about a bill for fish as being very high; twelve barrels herrings, $75; one barrel shads, $6.50.

Among the older citizens of Alexandria, recollections of the smells and sights of the fishing season, and stories they were told, are often heard. Each spring, the fishing activities around the wharves at Fishtown brought such thick clouds of flies into the center of town that windows were completely coated with the solid, moving mass of the winged insects. Little girls made up a verse about fish that they included in their rope-jumping games:

> Herring, herring, two for a penny,
> Ain't you 'shamed to eat so many.

The fishing season began in March and lasted about ten weeks. Shad and herring were caught in enormous quantities: as many as 160,000 fish were recorded in one haul. Farmers came from the back country and hauled home wagons loaded with fish, using the waste as fertilizer. A housewife could once buy a large shad for her family's dinner for a dime. One provident householder living on the edge of Alexandria noted in his

Fish, after wheat, was Alexandria's prime export in the early 1800's. The Potomac River was well-stocked with many types of fish, according to season. This charming plate, taken from "The Sportsman's Dictionary," reflects the great interest in fishing at that time.

This is a detail from an amusing print, one artist's conception of the many commercial fisheries that flourished along the Potomac River in George Washington's time. It is entitled *Funny Fish,* from the "General History of Druggs," published in 1712.

diary: "Went to town and brought out in my wagon 13,786 herrings, 50 shad, and 5 sacks salt for which I paid $5.50 per thousand, $9 per hundred, and $1.25 per sack. Struck the fish in salt this evening, in 4 hogsheads and 5 barrels."

Commercial processing and packing plants were built along both sides of the Potomac River. There was a fishery at Mount Vernon. Mason's grandson and namesake had several "striking houses" on property that the family owned opposite Gunston Hall. A plant building was about a hundred feet long and 3,000 barrels of fish could be cured at a time in each one.

In 1824 the dignitaries and citizens of the town prepared an elaborate reception in honor of the Marquis de Lafayette who came to Alexandria on a visit on October 24. A military escort met Lafayette's barouche, drawn by four matched grey horses, when it left Washington and accompanied the distinguished guest, the Secretary of State John Quincy Adams, and the others in the party into Alexandria. A grand arch reached across 100-foot wide Washington Street in the center of town. A live eagle, furnished by the Alexandria Museum, perched at the top of the arch. As Lafayette passed under the arch, the eagle flapped its wings and uttered a loud screech. The small boy at the window in a house facing the street holding the string to which the eagle was attached grinned mischievously.

At the dinner held at Gadsby's Tavern, Lafayette offered a toast: "The City of Alexandria—May her prosperity and happiness more and more realize the fondest wishes of our venerated Washington." Later that day, Lafayette paid a call on Mrs. Henry Lee, the widow of his old friend. The Hallowells, Mrs. Lee's next door neighbors, were standing at their door and for years afterward showed how the famous Frenchman bowed to them.

The more prosperous citizens became increasingly interested in educational and cultural activities. The Tuesday night lectures at the Lyceum were well attended, and hostesses planned their parties so as not to conflict with them. John Quincy Adams delivered a lecture at the Alexandria Lyceum during which he read the often-quoted sentence: "Man's nature requires, in order for him to fill his true sphere and be happy, three things—one fixed house, one wedded wife, and a belief in God."

The Alexandria Academy, which was unique in its day because it had no religious affiliation, served both free and pay students. Because it was a day school, many of the town's residents had the children of their friends who lived "in the country" as five-day-week boarders. In 1824, a Quaker schoolmaster, Dr. Benjamin Hallowell, opened a boarding school in a large house he rented on Oronoco Street.

There were many Quakers living in Alexandria at about this time. Their old letters and diaries that have survived are written in the speech of the plain people, "thee" and "thou" and a special terminology for the days of the week and the months of the year. Because they believed that the calendar names customarily used represented pagan religions, their Sunday schools are first-day schools, Tuesday night third-day evening, and October tenth-month in many Alexandria records.

Mrs. Lee's son, Robert, attended the Alexandria Academy for several years, and when he was preparing to enter West Point, studied mathematics under Dr. Hallowell. The Hallowell School was an immediate success. The roster for one year listed boys from fourteen different states and territories, South America, Cuba, and England. The school was later moved from Oronoco Street to the corner of Queen and Washington Streets, where it was enlarged by converting the adjacent sugar-house into a dwelling. Dr. Hallowell was so busy building and teaching that he spent his lunch time making quill pens. His students used up about a hundred pens a week, and he had no free time to devote to this chore.

Dr. Hallowell also gave private lessons. Angela Lewis, the daughter of Mr. and Mrs. Lawrence Lewis of Woodlawn, was one of his private students. The Lewis family moved into Alexandria for part of the year so that their children could attend school or receive private instruction from Alexandria teachers. Mrs. Lewis, the former Nellie Custis of Mount Vernon, took a keen interest in Angela's studies and always sat in the room to listen when Dr. Hallowell came to hear her daughter's recitations in English grammar and natural philosophy. Arch Hall, the Lewis' townhouse, has been moved from Alexandria, but was re-erected on Belmont Bay, not far from Gunston Hall.

The first American geography book was published in 1789 and soon afterward was in use in the Alexandria Academy. In the 1812 edition the author, Reverend Jedediah Morse, included a chapter on the District of Columbia with the figures from the 1810 census. At that time there were 8,208 people living in Washington, " . . . in five separate divisions or villages, one near the Capitol, one near the navy yard, one at Greenleaf's point, one near the President's house and one near Georgetown. . . ." Alexandria's population that year was 7,227; in 1800 it had been 4,971. Reverend Morse commented on the capital city's natural beauties and its central location ". . . about equidistant from the northern and southern extremity of the Union, and nearly so from the Atlantic to Pittsburg, . . ."

Among the boys attending classes during the second decade of the 1800's was John Gadsby's grandson, John Gadsby Chapman. This native son of Alexandria became a celebrated artist. One of his best known works is his mural, "The Baptism of Pocahontas," in the rotunda of the Capitol in Washington. Another famous painting by Chapman is "Mrs. Jane Washington and her children." Mrs. Washington's son, John Augustine Washington, junior, who appears in the painting as a child, was the last private owner of Mount Vernon.

When Mr. John A. Washington, junior, owned Mount Vernon he arranged to have an Alexandria excursion boat run from Washington to Mount Vernon for the convenience of the many visitors who came there. On one occasion, he hired the boat for a guest's pleasure. He took Jenny Lind, the famed Swedish singer, and his family up the Potomac to Washington. Except for the three-year period between 1862-65, and one year during World War II, excursion boats have been carrying sightseers between Washington and Mount Vernon ever since. Private and official parties also use the Mount Vernon wharf.

One river trip ended in a tragedy near Alexandria. Late in the afternoon of the last day of February, 1844, the townspeople heard the firing of a gun from the Potomac. Crowds rushed to the waterfront where the new warship, the *USS Princeton*, was dropping anchor. Only a few hours before, many in the crowd had waved gaily from the shore as the warship had sailed majestically past bound for Mount Vernon. Now they silently watched, shocked at the sight of the wounded being carried ashore, the air filled with the sound of women on the ship weeping over their dead.

The *USS Princeton* was the first propeller-built ship of the United States Navy, and was equipped

The USS *Princeton,* the first propeller-built ship of the United States Navy. It had a telescoping funnel and its two wrought-iron guns were the largest made up to this time.

with a telescoping funnel and armed with the two largest wrought-iron guns made up to this time. On board were select guests who had been invited to see the new ship and its guns. President John Tyler headed the list of high-ranking government officials who, with their wives and daughters, were in the party. Opposite Mount Vernon the guns were fired twice. Then, on the return trip and when the ship was below Alexandria, one of the guns was fired again and burst. Among those killed were two cabinet officers and a former New York State senator, David Gardiner. His daughter, Julia, fainted but revived as she was carried off the ship. Her struggles to free herself from the man's arms almost knocked both herself and the President of the United States, who was carrying her, into the Potomac River. Four months later Julia Gardiner became Mrs. John Tyler, mistress of the White House.

Almost everything of importance in Alexandria was connected in some way with the Potomac. The town's growth and the well-being of its citizens depended directly on the river. The townspeople thought of it as their lifeline to far-away world markets as well as nearby plantation neighbors. But the Potomac River failed to connect the Virginia section to the Maryland section of the capital city of Washington. It separated them.

In February 1801, when Alexandria ceased to be part of Virginia and the United States Congress assumed jurisdiction, the townspeople had expected great benefits. But the alliance was a disappointment from the outset. Real estate values soared in Washington but sales fell 25 per cent in three months in Alexandria. The priviso stipulating that no public buildings were to be erected on the Virginia side of the river was blamed in part for this. Some Alexandrians felt that their town was a forgotten corner of the District of Columbia. The taxes

The explosion of the "Peace-Maker" on board the USS *Princeton* on February 28, 1844.

levied on them by the Federal government caused much discontent. There were men in Alexandria who had helped govern themselves as residents of Virginia and who now considered themselves deprived of their Con-

175

stitutional rights. Alexandrians had no representation in the United States Congress, and there was much grumbling and whispered comparisons between their situation and that of the colonies under Great Britain.

As early as 1824 one group of Alexandria citizens tried to have their town retroceded to Virginia. After the great fire of 1827, Alexandrians invested heavily in canal building but their expectations for increased revenue from this source failed. Railroads took over the commerce planned for the canals and made them obsolete even before they were completed. The opening of the western lands lured young men from the town and the population, which was 8,218 in 1820, was only 8,241 in 1830. The Bank of Alexandria failed in 1834 and the United States government later purchased the building for $8,000 to use as a customs house. The panic of 1837, caused by over-expansion in canal building, speculation in western lands, and wildcat banking, brought about a nationwide crisis that continued into the 1840's. Alexandria merely existed during that period.

A petition for retrocession was finally drawn up and presented to Congress on February 3, 1846. On July 9, it was approved by an Act of Congress. That part of the state that had been ceded to the Federal government was returned to Virginia. As Alexandria County, it had been part of the District of Columbia for almost fifty years. Later, one section became Arlington County and Alexandria was chartered as a city.

Immediately after retrocession, Alexandria's prospects improved. In 1849 the Orange and Alexandria Railroad was organized. This railroad is now part of the Southern Railway System, which extends along almost 10,000 miles into practically every major city of the South. The Mount Vernon Cotton Factory, incorporated by an act of the General Assembly of Virginia in 1847, was doing well. The pottery business started by Benedict C. Milburn in 1841 and continued by his son grew rapidly, and examples of the work made by these fine artisans are collectors items. Furniture and agricultural implements were manufactured in the town. Handmade silver continued to be an important business, and improved as other businesses succeeded. During the years between 1850 and 1860 the population increased from 8,734 to 12,652. Alexandrians looked forward to a prosperous future. The next year the nation was at war.

Detail from the Advance Guard of the Grand Army of the United States crossing the Long Bridge over the Potomac, at 2 a.m., on May 24, 1861.

CHAPTER SEVENTEEN

The Death of Chivalry in War

This four year period, 1861-65, is the saddest in the town's history. These were the years of the war between the North and the South, a war with many names. It is officially designated as The War of the Rebellion. To Northerners, it is The Civil War. In Alexandria, and throughout the South, it is often called The War Between the States. America's great poet, Robert Frost, referred to it as "The Civil War Between the States." For the sake of brevity and also because it was recognized as the official name by the Civil War Centennial Commission, the Civil War is used in this book. That war began for Alexandrians in May, 1861.

President Abraham Lincoln and his family had been in the White House only a few weeks. A young man named Elmer E. Ellsworth, a former law student in Lincoln's Springfield, Illinois, law office, came to Washington on the presidential train. He hoped to get a position in the War Department. Lincoln recommended him for Chief Clerk but the position had been promised to another, and Lincoln then commissioned him a lieutenant in the First Dragoons, later the New York Eleventh Regiment.

Ellsworth first came to Lincoln's attention in 1860 when the young man led the United States Zouave Cadets through a spectacular drill in Springfield, eliciting from Lincoln the remark, "He is the greatest little man I ever met." Only five feet six inches tall, the spirited, dark haired, boyish looking, twenty-three-year-old Ellsworth had great personal fascination. He had wanted to be a soldier since he was a child but he could not afford to join one of the uniformed volunteer companies that were in vogue at the time. He was seventeen when the Crimean War broke out and was intrigued with the pictures of the colorful red, blue and gold uniforms and elaborate drill of the Zouaves, a unit of native troops fighting for the French in Algeria. He memorized books on military tactics, and when this became known, was invited to drill a group of young cadets. His expertise in military drills plus his magnetic personality were quickly recognized and he became the leader of the newly named United States Zouave Cadets. In 1860, after writing a manual of arms, Ellsworth and his Zouaves toured twenty cities in the East to compete with other drill companies. His men put on a spectacular performance at West Point. Their drill was also seen by President James Buchanan in Washington. Ellsworth put aside thoughts of a military career in order to help his parents financially and because he was engaged to be married, and came to Washington to look for work in a government department.

While the question of a government position for him was under discussion, Ellsworth, who had become a favorite with both the President and Mrs. Lincoln, was a frequent visitor at the White House and often played games with the two Lincoln boys, Willie and Tad. When the boys came down with the measles, Ellsworth caught them, too, and developed a very severe case of the disease. When President Lincoln issued a call for 75,000 volunteers on April 15, Ellsworth was still confined to his room at the Willard Hotel. Although weak, he left immediately for New York City, recruited a band of firemen, spent ten days intensively at work outfitting and drilling them, and brought the 1,100 men to Washington, where he quartered them in the Capitol. Dressed in the gaudy, bright costumes of Zouaves and armed with guns and knives, they delighted young boys and terrified old ladies as they marched through the streets of Washington.

Tension had been mounting steadily on both sides of the Potomac River that spring. Alexandrians anxiously followed the debates in Richmond, Virginia, on the question of whether or not their state should secede from the Union. On May 23, 1861, Virginians voted in the affirmative. Under cover of night, Federal troops quietly converged on Alexandria by land and by water. The old port town was stragetically situated on the river approach to Washington and its closeness was a threat to the safety of the capital city if it remained under Southern control. Besides, its railroad yards were an important supply center and distribution point for the South.

Colonel Ellsworth and his Zouaves were on board one of the three steamboats that reached Alexandria just before dawn on May 24. They landed under the protection of the Federal steamer *Pawnee* anchored in Alexandria harbor with its guns in position to fire on the town. It was five o'clock and most Alexandria citizens were asleep. In a low voice, Ellsworth ordered a company to destroy the railroad track that ran along the river's edge. Then, with five men, he hurried up King Street to cut the wires at the telegraph office. A short distance up the street stood a small hotel, the Marshall House. Tradition says that the young colonel had promised Mrs. Lincoln, who could see the Confederate flag flying over the hotel roof through a spyglass, that he would bring it back to her as a souvenir. On reaching the hotel, Ellsworth decided to stop and get the flag then. He raced up to the roof, his men taking the steps two at a time behind him, and cut the flag down from its pole. The noise on the stairs awakened the proprietor, Mr. James W. Jackson. Jackson, a devoted but hot-headed Southerner, had rashly boasted that the flag would never be taken down except over his dead body. As Ellsworth and his men came down the stairs, Jackson met them at the foot of the steps, gun in hand. Accounts of what happened then differ. According to one, Ellsworth held up the captured flag and said, "See, I have a trophy." Another version maintains that Ellsworth, intent on folding the flag, did not see Jackson, and was killed instantly by the shot from the hotel owner's gun. Corporal Francis E. Brownell of the Zouaves immediately shot Jackson, bayoneting his body as it fell. Then the Zouaves, carrying the body of their leader on their rifles, along with the flag for which he had given his life, returned to Washington. Colonel Ellsworth's body lay in state in the East Room of the White House, and President Lincoln and his family were the chief mourners at the funeral service held there. The young soldier's parents met their dead son, their last surviving child, in New York City and took him home to Mechanicsville, where he was buried with full military honors.

An old Currier & Ives print shows Colonel Elmer E. Ellsworth shot to death by Mr. James W. Jackson, proprietor of the Marshall House. Jackson is, in turn, killed by Corporal Francis E. Brownell. Ellsworth was a favorite with President and Mrs. Lincoln, and had promised Mrs. Lincoln the Confederate flag flying defiantly across the Potomac atop the Marshall House in Alexandria. Although Alexandria was quickly taken by the Union forces, the adventure ended tragically for Ellsworth.

Many Alexandrians became refugees for the four years of the Civil War as their town was taken over by troops. This old photograph shows soldiers in front of the Bank of the Old Dominion, Prince Street, circa 1863.

CHAPTER EIGHTEEN

Four
Years
of Conflict

Even before that 24th of May when Federal forces arrived in Alexandria, the town had taken on a war-like appearance. About 750 men, members of several Virginia militia companies, were quartered in Alexandria in hastily constructed barracks. Men in uniform mingled with the townspeople in the shops on King Street and cavalry galloped through the center of Washington Street. Early in May the mayor had warned the Alexandrians that it was dangerous for them to stay in the unfortified town and advised them to leave as quickly as possible. All during that month families broke up their homes. Many Alexandrians became refugees for the four years of the war. The family of the Reverend John P. McGuire, principal of the Episcopal High School for Boys, and Mrs. McGuire were among those who left.

The Protestant Episcopal Theological Seminary and the Episcopal High School are in the Seminary Hill area of Alexandria, on adjacent grounds. Both institutions dismissed their students early in May. Faculty wives packed linen, pictures, books, china, and silver. They covered the furniture and supervised taking carpets up and curtains down. They could hear, through the open windows, the drums beating in Washington, and see the Capitol in the distance, as they went about locking up whatever they could. On May 24, when word reached "The Hill" of the deaths in the Marshall House, Mrs. McGuire quickly packed as many trunks and boxes as their carriage would hold. She gave the household keys to the cook and instructed the servants to take care of the cows, the flower and vegetable gardens, and their Newfoundland dog. When the McGuire's came to the first crossroads, they stopped. After a few minutes, Dr. McGuire turned to his wife, saying, "It makes not the slightest difference which road we take: we might as well drive to the right hand as to the left, since nothing remains to us."

A few days later they were staying with friends at Chantilly, a Virginia town near what is now the Dulles International Airport. Mrs. McGuire's diary reads: "Mrs. General Lee has been with us for several days, and feels that she has left Arlington for an indefinite period. They removed their valuables, silver, etc., but the furniture is left behind." General Robert E. Lee had repeatedly urged his wife to leave Arlington, but she had put off doing so until the 18th, only a few days before the Union army crossed the Potomac River. On May 24, the Lee home was taken over by Federal soldiers on their march to Alexandria. Mrs. Lee saw Arlington once again, briefly. Dr. and Mrs. McGuire never returned to "The Hill."

Many Southern women expected the same chivalrous courtesies to which they were accustomed in normal

186

times. When Mrs. Lee, the former Mary Ann Randolph Custis, left Arlington for Richmond, Virginia, she stayed with friends or relatives along the way. She stopped for a visit at the White House in Kent County, Virginia, the home of the Custis family. Here she was in actual danger of capture by Federal troops. When she was finally persuaded to continue on her journey, she turned back to tack this note to the door:

"Northern soldiers who profess to reverence Washington, forbear to desecrate the home of his first married life, the property of his wife, now owned by her descendents.

(signed) A Grand-Daughter of Mrs. Washington"

Alexandria was taken over by Federal troops that May morning in 1861. The town was unfortified and had no way to resist occupation by the Union forces. When the harbor sentry signaled the approach of ships at dawn on the 24th, the Virginia militia companies met by prearranged plan in front of the Lyceum, at the intersection of Prince and Washington Streets. A monument marks the spot. Passing automobiles have hit the pedestal supporting the brooding Confederate soldier several times but Alexandrians ignore the repeated requests to move their soldier to another location. After each collision, they turn him once again to this original position, facing South. The alerted militia companies marched out of town and got safely aboard the trains that day but about thirty-five of the rear guard cavalry were captured.

The Federal army quickly occupied the vacated houses on "The Hill." Buildings that were in the way of the fortifications constructed around the town were destroyed. One of these was the home of General Samuel

Mary Lindsey, Alexandria; Library of Congress, Washington, D.C.

Upper Cameron Street, Alexandria. Part of the Lord Fairfax House is at
the right. On the far left is the childhood home of General Robert E. Lee.
The plaque on the wall quotes from the eulogy on Washington delivered
to the Congress of the United States by Lee's father, Colonel Henry Lee:
"First in war, first in peace, and first in the hearts of his countrymen. . . ."

188

Alexandria Library, Alexandria, Va.
Photo by Thomas T. Waterman

A detail of the Lord Fairfax House doorway shows the extraordinary workmanship lavished on Alexandria homes.

Arlington House, the home of General Robert E. Lee after his marriage, in 1864 (above), and under occupation by Union troops (right). It is now the Custis-Lee Mansion and has a commanding view of the Potomac River and Washington, D.C.

190

191

Photo by U.S. Signal Corps, Brady Collection, National Archives, Washington, D.C.

Alexandria was captured by Federal troops in May of 1861. Fortifications were quickly constructed around the town.

William Francis Smith, Alexandria

Lower Cameron Street, looking east, circa 1863. This is a typical photograph
of how Alexandria looked during The Civil War.

193

Cooper, the highest ranking officer in the Confederate army. The protestant Episcopal Theological Seminary became General George B. McClellan's headquarters and the Episcopal High School for Boys was turned into a hospital. The wooded hillsides on "The Hill" were cleared of trees. With nothing to obstruct them, the opposing armies in the Alexandria neighborhood could almost look into the muzzles of one another's guns. Some soldiers from Alexandria, part of a unit encamped on a hilltop behind the town, could see the chimneys of their own homes.

Alexandria warehouses and factories were used as Union armories and arsenals. Business buildings and private residences housed military and civil officers. Churches and schools were converted into hospitals and rest homes. Almost all shops and stores closed. Residents who took the oath of allegiance to the Federal government could support themselves by selling food, drink, etc., to the troops. Confederate money was worthless. Many men too old for military service left Alexandria to look for work so that they could support their families. All those who stayed on in the occupied town were cut off from news of the war and their loved ones at the front. The streets were unsafe, especially for women, who were in danger of meeting armed, and sometimes intoxicated, Union soldiers. One woman was murdered, and the guilty soldier was hanged at Fort Ellsworth, built on the hill where the Masonic National Memorial now stands.

The townspeople chafed under restrictions, even though some were for their own benefit. A nine o'clock curfew was enforced. Citizens were warned against gathering in groups. Their homes were subject to search and they themselves to arrest. Several leading businessmen, including a banker, were imprisoned. Christ Church

194

remained open throughout the war but a Federal chaplain officiated at services. Ministers of some of the other churches were subjected to indignities. One local minister who refused to include a prayer for the President was forcibly taken from the pulpit and led out of the church, with his small daughter clinging to his robes. Another minister had to ride the cowcatcher of a train carrying war materiel to the front so that Confederate soldiers would hold their fire as the cars passed through their lines.

An anecdote about Colonel Heros von Borcke, the Prussian officer in the Confederate army, reveals a little known side of General Robert E. Lee's character. A rumor of the death of Colonel von Borcke, General J.E.B. Stuart's chief of staff, had reached the governor of Virginia, who immediately notified Lee to send the body to Richmond for burial with full military honors. Lee replied: "Can't spare it. It's in pursuit of Stoneman." (General George Stoneman, U.S.A.)

An August 6th Alexandria diary entry reads: "Prince Napoleon passed through our lines today." Whether at peace or war, the United States continued to attract visitors from abroad, some as sightseers and others as participants.

Prince Napoleon and his wife, Princess Clotilde, with their retinue arrived in Washington the summer of 1861 on a tour of the United States. The Prince had planned to include the customary visit to George Washington's tomb but would have to pass through the lines of both armies on the way to Mount Vernon. President Lincoln suggested that he go down the Potomac by steamer as the best way to make the trip. Mrs. Lincoln had visited Mount Vernon that spring, by the same steamer that regularly carried the tourists. The Frenchman maintained that he preferred to go by the land route.

Mount Vernon was in a most singular situation throughout the war. As the battleground shifted, the estate was often between the camps of the Union and Confederate armies. Although patrols from the opposing forces would meet in the woodland surrounding Mount Vernon, both the Northern and Southern soldiers revered it as sacred ground.

President Lincoln had offered Prince Napoleon a bodyguard of 100 men, but the Prince had declined and set out with the six men in his party at dawn on an August day, in two carriages, to visit Mount Vernon. They crossed the bridge over the Potomac and passed long lines of white tents on the road they followed toward Alexandria. Sentries examined their pass at intervals. Seven miles beyond Alexandria the party came to the last Federal outpost, where fifty men were encamped. They had camouflaged their shelter and closed the road by felling two large trees, one from each side. After a hurried discussion, the soldiers decided that it would be easier to move the carriages than the tree trunks. They lifted the carriages to the other side of their road block while the unhitched horses took the long way around. A few miles beyond this outpost the Frenchmen came to the edge of a clearing. A handwritten sign on a board read: "Mount Vernon Alley." The rotting gate was open, and after walking for half an hour in a park turned into a forest, they reached the Mount Vernon buildings.

The last private owner of Mount Vernon, John A. Washington, junior, had moved out of the house in 1860, taking the furnishings with him. When the Mount Vernon Ladies' Association of the Union acquired the property, the only things that were left in the house that had belonged to George Washington when they bought it

196

Mount Vernon Ladies Association, Mount Vernon, Va.

Mount Vernon was often caught between the camps of the Union and Confederate troops during the Civil War. It was preserved largely through the courageous efforts of Miss Sarah C. Tracy, resident secretary of the Mount Vernon Ladies' Association of the Union. The Association had purchased the property a short time before the war and Miss Ann Pamela Cunningham, the Association's founder and first regent, felt that "the presence of a lady" would help save Washington's home from possible harm.

were the key to the Bastille, the globe in Washington's study, the model of Houdon's bust of Washington, six leather fire buckets, and three leather camp chests in bad repair. They could have done very little to furnish or restore the place in the short time before hostilities and nothing after the war began.

The party of Frenchmen saw a silent and apparently deserted house greatly in need of repairs set in dense woodland that seemed about to engulf it. There were some cabins near it and they caught glimpses of the servants living in them. The main house seemed deserted. They hesitated a moment before stepping through the doorway. At the same moment, a young woman appeared from somewhere in the house and welcomed them. Their hostess, small and dainty and obviously shy, was Miss Sarah C. Tracy, resident secretary of the Mount Vernon Ladies' Association of the Union, and she spoke fluent French. In answer to the Prince's question, she pointed out the path to Washington's tomb. Then she hurried into the kitchen to see about preparing a lunch for seven men from the limited supply of food on hand. She and the servants managed to have a meal ready for the visitors when they came back to the house.

After lunch and a tour of the house Miss Tracy gave the Prince a plant that had been growing near the tomb as a present for his wife. When the Frenchmen were ready to leave, they discovered that two of their horses were too tired to make the return trip. So the Prince and his companions traveled in a carriage drawn by the Mount Vernon mules as far as Alexandria, where they changed to horses.

The unexpected arrival of a prince was a minor crisis for Sarah Tracy during the four years of the war. Miss Ann Pamela Cunningham, the founder and first

In this early Civil War photo of Mount Vernon, Miss Sarah C. Tracy, resident secretary, is at the extreme left.

regent of Mount Vernon, asked her to stay on in the house when war broke out because she felt that "the presence of a lady" would protect Washington's beloved Mount Vernon. It did. But while protecting Mount Vernon, Miss Tracy herself was often in danger. She could hear the guns, both Southern and Northern, and soldiers from nearby outposts asked to see the house. A companion, Miss Mary McMackin, came to live with Sarah Tracy. There was also the superintendent of the estate, Mr. Upton H. Herbert of Alexandria. Lastly, there were a few workmen and the Negroes in the cabins. Practically all they had to eat came from the garden and the chicken house. There was very little money for food. During the fishing season, the two women often fished from the Mount Vernon pier for the main dish of a meal. One day Mary fell into the Potomac River. The demure Sarah glanced quickly around before she stepped out of her voluminous skirt and threw one end of it to her companion. Then, using the billowing garment as a lifeline, she pulled Mary to safety.

Miss Tracy supplemented their meager diet by bartering or selling the Mount Vernon vegetables and eggs. Armed with a military pass, she drove her horse and buggy to the market in Alexandria and to customers in Washington. When her pass had to be renewed, she went to the White House and saw President Lincoln about it. It was hazardous for a young woman to drive alone on these trips. In winter, she was often on the road to Mount Vernon after dark and was doubtless very much frightened of the soldiers posted along the way. The soldier might not recognize her or fire his gun by mistake. But the plucky Sarah continued to supply her customers with fresh vegetables and eggs.

When the Association bought Mount Vernon for $200,000 they paid for it in United States government bonds, and Mr. Washington deposited most of them with Burke & Herbert, bankers in Alexandria. In May 1861, Mr. Washington joined the Confederate army, and the same month the Federal army occupied Alexandria. The Mount Vernon sale was public knowledge and army officers went to the bank and demanded the bonds. Mr. John W. Burke had foreseen this possibility and moved the bonds to his house. He put the money bag in the bedroom closet, covering it with shoes and clothing. When the search party came to Mr. Burke's house, Mrs. Burke led the Federal officer upstairs. He pointed to the closet door and asked, "What is in there?" Mrs. Burke opened the door and answered, "It is my closet, as you can see for yourself." "It is not my wish to search a lady's closet," said the officer and shut the door.

Miss Tracy often stopped in to see her friends Mr. and Mrs. Burke if she was in their neighborhood. A few days after the money search affair, she paid them a visit before going on to Washington. As she was about to leave, Mr. Burke asked her to take a package along with her to the Riggs Bank there. She emptied her egg basket, put the package in the bottom, and then covered it with the eggs. At the bank, she emptied the contents of her basket on the desk of Mr. George Washington Riggs, Jr., saying as she did so that the package came from a friend across the river. Mr. Riggs slipped the package inside his desk and handed Miss Tracy the money due her for the Mount Vernon eggs.

Mr. John A. Washington was killed early in the war. Mrs. Washington had died the year before. The money that Miss Tracy carried to Washington in her egg basket supported their orphaned children. After the war, Sarah Tracy and Upton Herbert, the Mount Vernon superintendent whose brother was the junior partner of the banking firm, Burke & Herbert, were married and made their home near Alexandria.

Immediately following the first battle of the war, sometimes called the Battle of Bull Run (after the stream that runs through the battlefield) or the Battle of Manassas (after the nearby town), Alexandria became a hospital center. The first soldiers wounded in the war were brought to Alexandria by train. Cots were set up in public buildings, schools, churches, and even private homes. Temporary shelters and tents were put up in any open space. Convalescent soldiers and prisoners of war had to be housed in the town. Sanitary conditions were appalling. The situation was so bad in one camp that the soldiers nicknamed it Camp Misery. There are row upon row of thousands of headstones marking the graves of Union soldiers buried in the Alexandria National Cemetery at the end of Wilkes Street, many of them unknown soldiers.

In the spring of 1862, troops and supplies in extraordinary numbers were shipped southward from the Alexandria waterfront for the Peninsula Campaign. Trainloads of soldiers arrived in the town to board the steamers dotting the Potomac River. Tons of baggage were hoisted on board with them. A derrick lifted a train engine onto a waiting schooner. Artillery horses were loaded in the same manner. The freight cars were to be unloaded on the rails further south, along with the engine. Barges carrying guns, gun carriages, and other war materiel accompanied every flotilla shuttling between Alexandria and Fortress Monroe. More than a hundred thousand men, thousands of horses, and innumerable pieces of battle equipment moved down the river on steamers, barges, and schooners in a single month. The loading scenes became commonplace as they continued during the war years.

Alexandria became a hospital center following the Battle of Bull Run. Thousands of headstones in the Alexandria National Cemetery mark the graves of the Union soldiers buried there, many of them unknown soldiers.

In June, 1863, Alexandria was selected as the capital of "The Restored Government of Virginia," a further blow to the pride of its citizens loyal to the South. The western part of Virginia had joined the Union and West Virginia was admitted as a separate state. Alexandria was one of several Virginia areas under Federal control. The purpose of the "Restored Government" was to reclaim the Virginia state government for the Federal government. The executive was Governor Francis H. Pierpont, and he chose the building at 415 Prince Street in Alexandria as his headquarters. This rump government remained in Alexandria until the end of the war.

CHAPTER NINETEEN

Aftermath of the Occupation

The Civil War ended on April 9, 1865. Refugees began returning from elsewhere in Virginia, other states, and Canada. Many Southerners remained in Canada until July 4, 1868 when President Andrew Johnson proclaimed a general amnesty. Among them was the Special Commissioner of the Confederate States of America to Great Britain, James Murray Mason, a grandson of George Mason of Gunston Hall. Commissioner Mason brought his family to Alexandria. He spent the last months of his life at Clarens, an estate adjoining that of his brother-in-law, General Samuel Cooper, on "The Hill."

On May 3, 1869 a steamer docked at Alexandria and General Robert E. Lee stepped off. This was his first visit to his home town in eight years. As he walked the few blocks to a relative's house, many people recognized him and stopped to greet him. Later, an informal reception was arranged in his honor at the hotel, now the Carlyle Apartments, built on the North Fairfax Street side of the Carlyle House. Half the town filed past him in a continuous line for two hours. After the reception, General Lee drove up to "The Hill" to call on General Samuel Cooper and visit with the boys at the Episcopal High School. His carriage drawn by a pair of handsome greys stopped often along the two-mile ride. Later he wrote, "There is no community to which my affections more strongly cling than that of Alexandria, composed of my earliest and oldest friends, my kind schoolfellows, and faithful neighbors."

According to tradition, General Lee was seen peeking over the garden fence of his boyhood home during this visit, and when asked what he was looking for, said that he just wanted to see if the snowballs were in bloom. They were, and they still bloom in May at 607 Oronoco Street, the street that predates the founding of the historic old town.

At the end of the Civil War, Alexandrians faced the gigantic task of rebuilding their town as a commercial center after four years of occupation. There was little money with which to finance such an undertaking. The impoverished citizens who had stayed in the town were augmented by refugees who had even less than they had. Stores and ships displayed secondhand clothing and junk which overflowed into the streets. Shabbily dressed women moved from one pile of used garments to another, endlessly turning them over as they looked for something suitable for their children to wear.

The one day in the week that many Alexandrians looked forward to was Sunday, when they could visit with old friends in the churchyard. Everyone who could manage to be decently clothed attended church. Once again the children's voices chorused "Amen" from the

The Robert E. Lee house on Oronoco Street, Alexandria. It was from this house that the South's great military leader left for West Point.

corner seats on either side of the chancel at Christ Church. This old custom has given these church seats their name, the amen corners.

A major Alexandria industry that had continued active during the Civil War years was the Orange and Alexandria Railroad built just before the War. When the Federal government took over the railroad, the car shops in Alexandria were put to use for the United States Military Railroad. Work was begun late in 1863 inside the military stockade on a private car for President Lincoln. The handsome railway car was completed in February, 1865. Inside and out, from the luxurious furnishings to the freshly painted American eagle in the oval panel on each side of the car, it was the pride of the military officials. The trial ride was set for April 15th. But the honored guest died early that morning. He had been shot the evening before in his box at Ford's Theatre by John Wilkes Booth. The dead President's Alexandria-built private railway car made its first and only official journey in a funeral train. Draped in black cloth, it carried the bodies of the President and his young son, Willie, from Washington to Springfield, Illinois, for burial. (In 1918, when the car was on exhibition, it was destroyed by a fire that started on the grass plot on which it stood.)

Many Alexandrians went to work for the railroads after the War. The Orange and Alexandria changed its name and ownership several times and became part of the Southern Railway when that company was organized in 1894, but the Richmond, Fredricksburg, and Potomac, still operates under that name.

In Honor of Washington

Another rail transportation system was inaugurated during the last decade of the 19th century. In 1892 the electric-powered train between Alexandria and Washington was extended on a single track from Alexandria to Mount Vernon. There were five side-tracks built along the route. (These side-tracks form the overlook points along the Potomac River on the George Washington Memorial Boulevard constructed in the 1930's. The roadbed of the railway was absorbed into the parkway.) The two-car train waited on the sidetrack until the cars coming from the opposite direction passed, leaving a clear track ahead. Later, this hourly service on the single track was expanded into a twenty-minute service on a double track. A parlor car for distinguished guests on a visit to Mount Vernon was added to the customary two-coach and freight car train when necessary. This elegant car, outfitted with bench-like seats upholstered in velvet, with carpets and curtains, and decorated with mahogany

209

Railroad tunnel along Wilkes Street, Alexandria.

panels, and the regular train service of the Washington, Alexandria & Mount Vernon Railway Company, remained in use until buses began operating over the boulevard completed in 1932.

The 200th anniversary of Washington's birth that year inaugurated a number of projects in and near Alexandria. One that died in the planning stage was the reconstruction of Belvoir, the Fairfax family home, but the most prominently situated structure in Alexandria, the George Washington Masonic National Memorial, was dedicated that bicentennial year.

The idea for an enduring memorial to Washington was proposed more than thirty years before then, at a meeting of prominent Masons in Alexandria, with the members of Alexandria-Washington Lodge No. 22 as hosts. Washington had been the first Master of Alexandria Lodge No. 22 (which later changed its name to include his), and the Lodge owned many Washington relics. The Lodge Room was originally in the City Hall in Alexandria, where a fire in 1871 destroyed a number of these relics. On view at the George Washington Masonic National Memorial Building are Washington's Masonic apron, which he wore at the laying of the cornerstone of the Capitol in Washington, the silver-and-ivory trowel he used at that ceremony, and the chair that he presented to the Lodge. A letter that Washington wrote a few weeks before he died is also preserved there. The customary complimentary ticket to the Alexandria balls had been sent to him and Mrs. Washington, and in acknowledgement his letter reads:

Mount Vernon
12th November, 1799.

Gentlemen: Mrs. Washington and myself have been honored with your polite invitation to the

211

Detail from Benjamin H. Latrobe's drawing of the procession of Alexandria Lodge No. 22 escorting George Washington to the cornerstone laying of the United States Capitol, September 18, 1793.

Assemblies in Alexandria this winter, and thank you for this mark of your attention. But, alas! our dancing days are no more. We wish, however, all those who relish so agreeable and innocent an amusement, all the pleasure the season will afford them. And I am, Gentlemen,

Your most obedient and obliged
humble servant,
Geo. Washington.

The design for the Masonic Memorial building is reminiscent of Egyptian architecture. Because of this resemblance, and the fact that the town is called Alexandria, many people erroneously believe that the town was named for Alexandria in Egypt, instead of for the Alexander family. There is a connection between the Egyptian city and the building. It was designed after the Pharos Lighthouse, one of the Seven Wonders of the Ancient World, which was built on an island in the Bay of Alexandria, Egypt. The president of the George Washington Masonic National Memorial Association accidentally met a New York architect on a train. The architect made a rough pencil sketch as they talked about the proposed building. The only difference between that original sketch and the Memorial as it appears today are a few changes made in the top of the structure.

The Assemblies, to which the Washington letter that is on view at the Masonic Memorial refers, were held at Gadsby's Tavern. The Tavern had also been affected by the general decline in the town after the Civil War. The hotel closed in 1879, and the property was used as an auction house and then as miserable tenements for the poorest families. In 1917, when the two old buildings seemed about to be destroyed, the owners sold the ballroom in the larger building to the Metropolitan Museum of Art of New York, where it was installed in the American Wing.

Shortly after this, the citizens of Alexandria organized a committee to buy Gadsby's Tavern for the Alexandria Post No. 24, the American Legion, instead of erecting a monument honoring the men of World War I. The initial payment was made from the proceeds of a street carnival, complete with lion cages and shooting ranges, plus substantial contributions from private individuals. The American Legion subsequently paid off the mortgage by installing slot machines in the buildings. In 1932, Gadsby's Tavern and City Hotel, Incorporated, was chartered. Five of the nine directors of the corporations are members of the American Legion. A number of civic and patriotic organizations and private individuals have restored the two buildings and furnished the rooms.

CHAPTER TWENTY-ONE

From Old Town to New City

Two events important to Alexandria occurred in 1932: the George Washington Bicentennial Celebration and the influx of New Deal residents. The many new government departments set up by President Franklin D. Roosevelt brought a large number of people to Washington to staff them. When the housing shortage in the nation's capital became acute, some of these New Dealers settled in Alexandria. Their stories of its charm enticed their friends to move across the Potomac and ended the quiescent period for the old seaport town.

Modern Alexandria dates from the 1930's. The town had become a city in 1920 and the corporate limits were extended to an area of seven and a half square miles in 1930. (Alexandria is double that size today.)

In 1932, the city gained impetus from projects connected with the George Washington Bicentennial observances. But the Great Depression delayed progress

215

The old-time charm that attracted many new residents to Alexandria in the 1930's is here illustrated in the brick paved street leading towards Christ Church. The Lord Fairfax House is to the far right.

216

supported by the city government. The first Federal government workers who had come to live in Alexandria at the beginning of the Franklin D. Roosevelt Administration were greatly augmented during World War II. They took over a number of the old houses on lower Prince Street, Sea Captains' Row, and fixed them up to make them livable. These early restorations initiated an interest in buildings elsewhere in the city, both public and private.

The Ramsay House, on the northwest corner of King and Fairfax Streets, was an early project of the city government. George Washington's Town House, at 508 Cameron Street, was privately built and is a reconstruction of the original. Promotional campaigns have been launched to attract tourists to George Washington's Hometown, halfway between the city of Washington and Mount Vernon. Business establishments have been invited to join historic-minded citizens in preservation and restoration, and the economic benefits to commerce and industry were emphasized.

Alexandria is still a port of entry and has a customs house to handle that part of its trade that is international. Tobacco, wheat, and flour have given place to almost a hundred diverse products, among them metal and wood awnings, cast stone, cinder blocks, concrete pipes, chemicals, dairy products, paper cups, electronic equipment, mattresses, neon signs, ornamental and other iron works, furniture, fertilizers, ice cream, and ice. Refrigerator cars are rebuilt in Alexandria, which has one of the largest icing stations on the eastern seaboard for ice cars and trucks. Warehousing is a specialty: a terminal of 150,000 square feet houses the enormous rolls of newsprint paper imported from abroad to supply all the daily newspapers in the Washington metropolitan area.

Lee Street from the Potomac River. The street was re-named in honor of General Robert E. Lee, who grew up in Alexandria.

The Mount Vernon Guards, a fife and drum corps of young boys, participate in historic and patriotic events in the Alexandria area.

These large and varied industries have increased Alexandria's population from less than 25,000 in 1930 to approximately 118,000 in 1969. It is predicted that there will be 150,000 people living in the city by the close of the 20th century.

In spite of this industrial expansion, many of the small business houses along the streets of old Alexandria had not kept pace with the changing times. Lack of parking space was chiefly blamed for this. The suburban type of shopping center was drawing the people away from the city stores. By the early 1960's, King Street, Alexandria's main shopping street, was sadly in need of revitalizing.

On June 13, 1963, the City Council approved an Urban Renewal Project for Alexandria. After many delays caused by differences among the various citizen groups, Phase I, covering two business blocks and known as the Gadsby Project, was dedicated on June 2, 1966. The landscaped Market Square, on the site of the colonial market place, with a seventy-five-foot square pool and illuminated fountain, has underground parking for 236 cars on two levels beneath it. The Tavern Square, a completely new block of buildings except for the two adjoining structures that form Gadsby's Tavern, is an office and retail store complex. It, too, has a two-level parking garage underground for more than 200 vehicles.

The modern shops are in sharp contrast to the old store-front buildings displaying antique furniture and 18th-century silver along lower King Street. Alexandria's main street ends at a dockside building, a former tobacco warehouse, now stocked with household items imported from all over the world for the discerning shopper's selection. The contrast between old and new is especially evident in the many avant-garde galleries and

220

Photo by Don Heinemann, Alexandria City Manager s Office
The Market Square in Alexandria today.

studios. In recent years, ultra-modern artists have settled in the quaint old town and are as much at home as the descendants of the original families. Once again an appropriate toast is George Washington's: "Prosperity to the town and the citizens of Alexandria."

The Confederate Soldier Memorial at the intersection of Washington &
Prince Streets, Alexandria, on the direct route from Washington to Mount
Vernon.

Appendix

LAND PATENT ISSUED TO
MISTRESS MARGARET BRENT
IN 1654

To all etc. Whereas etc. Now know ye that I the said Rich. Bennett, Esq., etc. give & grant unto Mts. Margt. Brent Seven Hundred Acres of land Scit. in Westmorland County within ye freshes of Potomack River beginning at ye mouth of Hunting Creek and Extending along ye said Creek West by North 320 poles to a branch thereof from thence North by East 350 poles from thence East by South to Potomack River and along the said River to ye place where the tract of land first began being the mouth of Hunting Creek South by West 350 poles. The said land being due unto the said Mts. Margt. Brent by and for the transportation of fourteen persons into the Colony etc. to have And to hold etc. Yielding and paying etc. which payment etc. dated ye 6th of September 1654.

John Rainalls	James Donnell
Wm. Bonee	Wm. Wright
Robt. Lawrence	James Bryce
David Hollin	Rich. Conniers
Walter Donell	Rich. Coleman
Wm. Burt	James Ramsy
Bryan Morse	John Major

(from PATENTS, Book No. 3,
1652-1655, page 275.
Virginia State Archives,
Richmond, Va.)

224

PHOTOCOPY OF
LAND PATENT ISSUED TO
MISTRESS MARGARET BRENT
In 1654

PATENT OF 1654 REISSUED TO
MARGARET BRENT
In 1662

To all etc. Whereas etc. Know ye That I the said Sir William Berkeley Knight Governor etc. give and grant unto Margarett Brent Seven hundred Acres of Land in Westmorland County in the Freshes of Patomack River Beginning at the mouth of Hunting Creek & Extending along the said Creek West by North Three hundred and twenty poles to a branch thereof from thence North by East Three hundred and fifty poles from thence East by South to Potomack River and along the said River to the place where this Tract of Land first Began: being the mouth of Hunting Creek South by West Three hundred and fifty poles. The said Land being formerly granted to the said Brent by Patent dated the Sixth day of September One thousand Six hundred and fifty four, and now renewed in his Majesties name etc. To Have and To Hold etc. To be Held etc. Yielding and paying etc. provided etc. Dated the twentieth of November One thousand six hundred and sixty two.

(from PATENTS, Book No. 5,
1661-1666, vol. 1, pp. 1-340.
Virginia State Archives,
Richmond, Va.)

PHOTOCOPY OF
PATENT OF 1654 REISSUED TO
MARGARET BRENT
IN 1662

LAND PATENT ISSUED TO
ROBERT HOUSING (sic)
IN 1669

To all etc. Now hear etc. Now know ye that I the said Sir William Berkeley Kngt. Governor etc. give and grant unto Mr. Robt. Howsing Six thousand acres of land Scituate lying and being upon the freshes of Potomack River on the west side thereof above the dividing branches of the same beginning at an old oake standing by a small branch or arm of water neare opposite to a small island commonly called and known by the name of my Lords Island extending down the Potomack River various courses 3152 poles making a Southerly bend to a pohickory standing at the north point of a Creek called by the English Indian Cabin Creek which Creek divides this land and a tract of land surveyed for Jno. Washington from the said pohickory NW by W on the said Creek and varied branches 520 poles from thence etc. 1940 poles finally E 720 poles to the said oake begun all including and all small creeks or inlets for the said quantity. The said land being due for bringing of 120 persons to have and to hold etc. to be held etc. yielding and paying etc. dated etc. one and twentieth day of October 1669.

(from PATENTS, Book No. 6,
1666-1679, vol. 1, pp. 1-350.
Virginia State Archives,
Richmond, Va.)

PHOTOCOPY OF
LAND PATENT ISSUED TO
ROBERT HOUSING (sic)
IN 1669

THE FOUNDING ACT OF ALEXANDRIA

An act for erecting a town
at Huntington Creek Warehouse,
in the County of Fairfax
(Passed in the year 1748)

Whereas it hath been represented to this present General Assembly that a Town at Hunting Creek Warehouse on Potomac River, would be commodious for trade and navigation, and tend greatly to the ease and advantage of the frontier inhabitants, Be it therefore enacted by the Lieutenant Governor, Council and Burgesses of this present General Assembly, and it is hereby enacted by the authority of the same, that within four months after the passing of this act, sixty acres of land, parcel of the lands of Philip Alexander, John Alexander and Hugh West, situate lying and being on the south side of Potomac River, about the mouth of Great Hunting Creek and in the County of Fairfax, shall be surveyed and laid out by the surveyor of the said County, beginning at the mouth of the first branch above the warehouses, and extend down the meanders of the said River Potomac to a point called middle point, and thence down the said River ten poles; and from thence by a line parallel to the dividing line, between John Alexander's land and Philip Alexander, and back into the woods for the quantity aforesaid: and the said sixty acres of land so be surveyed and laid out, shall be, and is hereby vested in the Right Honorable Thomas Lord Fairfax, the Honorable William Fairfax, Esqr., George Fairfax, Richard Osborn, Laurence Washington, William Ramsey, John Carlyle, John Pagan, Gerard Alexander and Hugh West, of the said County of Fairfax, gentlemen, and Philip Alexander of the County of Stafford, gentleman, and their successors in trust for the several purposes hereinafter mentioned. And the said Thomas Lord Fairfax, William Fairfax, George Fairfax, Richard Osborne, L. Washington, William Ramsey, John Carlyle, John Pagan, Gerard Alexander, Hugh West and Philip Alexander are hereby constituted and appointed directors and trustees for designing, building, carrying on, and maintaining the said town upon the land aforesaid: and the said trustees and directors or any six of them, shall have power to meet as often as they shall think necessary, and shall lay out the said sixty acres into lots and streets not exceeding half an acre of ground in each lot: and also set apart such portions of the said land for a market place, and public landing as to them shall seem convenient: and, when the said town shall be so laid out, the said directors and trustees shall have full power and authority to sell all the said lots, by public sale or auction, from time to time, to the highest bidder, so as no person shall have more than two lots, and when any such lots shall be sold, any two of the said trustees shall and may, upon payment of the purchase money, by some sufficient conveyance or conveyances, convey the fee-simple estate of such lot or lots to the purchaser or purchasers; and he or they or his or their heirs or assigns, respectively, shall and may forever thereafter peaceably and quietly have, hold, possess and enjoy, freed and discharged from all right, title, claim, interest and demand whatsoever of the said Philip Alexander, John Alexander and Hugh West, and the heirs and assigns of them respectively, all persons whatsoever claiming by, from or under them or either of them. *Provided nevertheless*, That the said trustees and directors, after deducting sufficient to reimburse the charge and expense of surveying and laying out the said lots, shall pay or cause to be paid, to the said Philip Alexander, John Alexander and Hugh West all the money arising by the sale

231

of the said lots according to their respective rights therein.

And be it further enacted, by the authority aforesaid, That the grantee or grantees of every such lot or lots to be sold or conveyed in the said town, shall within two years next after the date of the conveyance of the same, erect, build and finish on each lot so conveyed, one house of brick, stone or wood well framed of the dimensions of twenty feet square, and nine feet pitch, at the least or proportionately thereto if such grantee shall have two lots contiguous, with a brick or stone chimney; and the said directors shall have full power and authority to establish such rules and orders for the more regular placing the said houses as to them shall seem meet, and if the owner of any such lot shall fail to pursue and comply with the directions herein prescribed for the building and finishing one or more house or houses thereon, then such lots upon which such houses shall not be so built and finished shall be revested in the said trustees, and shall and may be sold and conveyed to any other person or persons whatsoever, in the manner before directed, and shall revest and be again sold as often as the owner or owners shall fail to perform, obey, and fulfil the directions aforesaid, and the money arising from the sale of such lots as shall be revested and sold as aforesaid shall be, by the said trustees from time to time, applied to such public use for the common benefit of the inhabitants of the said town as to them shall seem most proper; and if the said inhabitants of said town shall fail to obey and pursue the rules and orders of the said directors in repairing and mending the streets, landings, and public wharfs, they shall be liable to the same penalties as are inflicted for not repairing the highways in this colony. And for continuing the succession of the said trustees and directors, until the governor of this colony shall incorporate some other persons by letters patent, under the great seal of this colony to be one body politic and corporate, to whom the government of the said town shall be committed.

Be it further enacted, That in case of the death of the said directors or of their refusal to act, the surviving or other directors or the major part of them, shall assemble and are hereby empowered from time to time by instrument in writing, under their respective hands and seals, to nominate some other person or persons, being an inhabitant or freeholder of the said town, in the place of him so doing or refusing, which new director or directors so nominated and appointed shall from thenceforth have the like power and authority in all things relating to the matters herein contained, as if he or they had been expressly named and appointed in and by this act: and every such instrument and nomination shall, from time to time, be recorded in the books of the said directors.

And Be it further enacted, by the authority aforesaid, That the said town shall be called by the name of Alexandria.

And Be it further enacted, by the authority aforesaid, That it shall not be lawful for any person whatsoever, to erect or build, or cause to be erected or built in the said town, any wooden chimneys: and if any wooden chimney shall be built contrary to this act it shall and may be lawful for the Sheriff of the said County of Fairfax, and he is hereby required from time to time, to cause all such wooden chimneys to be pulled down and demolished.

And Be it further enacted, by the authority aforesaid, That no person whatsoever residing in the said town shall keep any swine running at large within the bounds thereof; and that it shall and may be lawful for any person whatsoever, to kill or destroy the same, and immediately give notice to the owner or owners thereof. *Provided always,* that nothing in this act shall be construed to prohibit Persons driving hogs for sale in or through the said town, or to prohibit Persons residing near the said town from letting their hogs run at large.

The Clerk of the House of Delegates having died since the last session of Assembly, and there being no person especially appointed to discharge the duties of that office, I do hereby certify as Lieutenant Governor (in the absence of the Governor) that the foregoing is a true copy of an Act of Assembly, passed in the year one thousand seven hundred and forty eight.

Given under my hand at Richmond,
this 12th day of October, 1795.
JAMES WOOD.

Pages 533-535, "The Acts of Congress, In Relation to the District of Columbia from July 16, 1790, to March 4, 1831, inclusive and of the Legislatures of Virginia and Maryland with Preliminary Notes of the proceedings of the Congress, Under the Confederation, etc., etc."

By William A. Davis, Washington City (Published and) printed by Wm. A. Davis, Pennsylvania Avenue, 1831.

MINUTES OF AN EARLY COUNCIL MEETING IN ALEXANDRIA

At a Council held at the
Camp at Alexandria in
Virginia April 14th, 1755.

Present
His Excellency Edward Braddock Esqr. General &
Commander in Chief of his Majestys Forces in North
America.

The Honoble. Augustus Keppel Esqr. Commander
in chief of his Majestys Ships and Vessels in North
America.

The Honble. William Shirley Esqr. The Honble.
Robert Dinwiddie Esqr. The Honble. James De Lancey
Esqr. The Honble. Horatio Sharpe Esqr. The Honoble.
Robt. Hunter Morris Esqr.

The Generals Commission having been read and
the Articles of his Instructions from his Majesty relating
to a common Fund to be established in the Colonies for
carrying on the services under the Generals direction,
and also the article relating to the measures to be taken
for engaging the Indians in his Majesty's Interest. His
Excellency the General made the following proposals.

1st   That a fund should be established conform-
able to his Instructions above-mentioned and to sir
Thomas Robinsons Letter to the several Governors
dated October 26, 1754.

2d   It being of the utmost importance that the five
Nations of Indians and their Allies should be gained and
secured to the British Interest, that a proper person
should be sent with full powers from him to treat with
them, and that Colonel Johnston, appearing to his Ex-

cellency the fittest person for that purpose, should be employed in it.

And in order to promote the success of the Treaty, the General proposed that presents should be made to the said Indians in which he desired the opinion of the Council as to the value to which the said presents should be made, and the manner of their being Supplied.

3d His Excellency acquainted the Council that he proposed to attack the French Forts at Crown point and Niagara and desired their Opinion whether it was advisable that the Reduction of Crown point should be undertaken with the forces agreed to be Supplied by the Several Colonies concerned in it amounting in the whole to 4400 Men and whether it was their opinion that Colonel Johnston was a proper person to Command in Chief the said service.

4th His Excellency considering the Fort at Oswego as a Post of the greatest importance for facilitating the proposed attack of Niagara, and securing the retreat of the Troops to be employed in that service, and having been informed of Its present Defenceless condition & of the weakness of its Garrison acquainted the Council that he should order it to be reinforced by the two Independent Companies of New York and two Companies of Sir William Pepperels Regiment, and desired to have their opinion whether it would not be proper to build one or more Vessels upon the Lake Ontario for asserting his Majesty's right to that Lake as well as for a Security to the Forces to be employed in the attack of Niagara, and of what burthen or Force the said Vessels should be.

The Members of the Council having taken into Consideration these several matters in the order proposed by the General. The Governors present acquainted his Excellency that they had severally made application to their respective Assemblies for the establishment of the common fund proposed, but had not been able to prevail upon 'em to agree to it, and gave it as their unanimous opinion that such a Fund can never be established in the Colonies without the aid of Parliament. They likewise declared that having found it impracticable to obtain in their respective governments their proportions expected by his Majesty towards defraying the expense of his service in North America, that they were unanimously of opinion that it should be proposed to his Majesty's Ministers to find out some method of compelling them to do it and of Assessing the several Governments in proportion to their respective abilities, their shares of the whole money already furnished and which it shall be thought proper for them to furnish towards the General expence of his service. They also assured the General that they would still continue to use their utmost endeavours to raise all possible supplies but were unanimously of Opinion that the Kings Service in the Colonies and the carrying on of the present Expedition must be at a stand unless the General shall think proper to make use of his credit upon the Government at Home to defray the expence of all the Operations under his direction.

The Members of the Council likewise agreed that it was highly necessary to send some person with full powers from the General to treat with the five Nations of Indians and to secure them and their Allies to the British Interest and that Coll. Johnston was the fittest man to be employed in that Business and for that purpose that the Sum of £800 Sterl should be paid into his hands to be laid out by him in such Commodities as he should judge most proper for the Northern and Western Indians £500 of which should be employed for the five Nations and their Allies and £300 for the Western Indians to be given at Oswego. And as to the manner of supplying the presents the several Govrs. agreed that if the General for the sake of Dispatch thinks proper to advance the money the Colonies ought to replace it according to the proportions settled in the Plan of Union by the Commissioners at Albany last year together with all contingent Charges attending it, and that it was their opinion that the several Governments would readily consent to do it within the space of three months.

The Council expressed their Approbation of the Attack proposed by the General upon Crown point and Niagara as being undoubted encroachments made by the French upon his Majestys Dominions in America and gave it as their Unanimous Opinion that Coll. Johnston was the properest person to have the Command of the Expedition against Crown point. They also agreed to the necessity of strengthening the Fort and reinforcing the Garison at Oswego, and advised the building of two Vessels of sixty Tons upon the Lake Ontario with all possible Dispatch according to a Draught to be sent by Commodore Keppel who desired that an account might be laid before him of the cost of 'em and undertook to defray it and it was agreed that the direction of the affair should be Committed to Govern. Shirley.

It was likewise unanimously agreed that in case of the Reduction of Fort Duquesne whatever Garison the General should think proper to leave there, should be maintained, and the expence of additional works which he should think necessary to make there, should be defrayed by the Governments of Virginia Maryland, and Pennsylvania, and that if the General should think it necessary to build a fort upon Lake Erie, and to order one or more Vessels to be built for the Defence of that

Lake, the expence attending both those measures should likewise be defrayed by those three Governments.

Examined

W. Shirley Secrty.

from:
THE DOCUMENTARY HISTORY OF THE
STATE OF NEW YORK
Arranged under direction of the
Hon. Christopher Morgan, Secretary of State.

By E. B. O'Callaghan, M.D.

Volume II. Albany: Weed, Parsons & Co.,
Public Printers
1849
Pages 648-651.

(original source: Manuscripts of
Sir William Johnson, Bart.,
Major General of the English Forces
in North America—on file in the
Secretary of State's Dept. Albany)

Bibliography

About Tobacco. Privately published: Lehman Bros., 1955.

A Hornbook of Virginia History comp. and ed. by J. R. V. Daniel, Division of History, Virginia Dept. of Conservation & Develop., Richmond, 1949.

"Alexandria, Alexandria County, Virginia." *Social Statistics of Cities: 1880.* Washington, D.C., Government Printing Office.

Alexandria Chamber of Commerce, publications.

Alexandria City, Arlington County, and Fairfax County, Virginia, Courthouse Records: Deed Books and Will Books.

Alexandria Gazette. 1784-1967.

Alexandria Urban Renewal Commission Publications, 1967.

Ambler, Charles H. *Francis H. Pierpont.* Chapel Hill, N.C.: University of North Carolina Press, 1937.

Andrews, Marietta Minnigerode. *Memoirs of A Poor Relation.* New York: Dutton & Co., 1927.

Andrews, Matthew Page, *History of Maryland.* Garden City, N.Y.: Doubleday & Co., 1929.

Antiques. February 1945 (issue devoted to Alexandria). New York: Straight Enterprises, Inc., 1945.

Arlington Historical Magazine. Arlington Historical Society, Arlington, Va. "Assumption of State Debts and Removal of the Seat of Government to the Potomac." *Jeffersonian Cyclopedia,* edited by John P. Foley. New York: Funk & Wagnalls Co., 1900.

Avery, Elroy M. *A History of the United States and Its People.* Cleveland: Burrows Bros., 1908.

Bailey, Thomas A. *The American Pageant: A History of the Republic.* Boston: D.C. Heath & Co., 1956.

Baker-Crothers, Hayes. *Virginia and the French and Indian War.* Chicago: University of Chicago Press, 1928.

Beirne, Rosamond R. and Scarff, J. H. *William Buckland: 1734-1774.* Baltimore: Maryland Historical Society, 1958.

Bennington, Edw. N. "Roads to Mount Vernon." *Virginia Cavalcade,* Winter 1960-61.

Braddock's Defeat. Edited by Chas. Hamilton. Oklahoma: University of Oklahoma Press, 1959.

Brandt, Beverly Seehorn. *The Alexandria, Virginia, Library: Its History, Present Facilities, and Future Program.* A study. Alexandria: 1951.

Brockett, F. L. *The Lodge of Washington.* Alexandria: Geo. W. French, 1876.

Brockett, F. L. and Rock, Geo. W. *A Concise History of the City of Alexandria, Virginia from 1669 to 1883, with A Directory of Reliable Business Houses in the City.* Alexandria: Gazette Book & Job Office, 1883.

Browne, Charlotte. "Journal of a Voyage from London to Virginia 1754." Photostat. Manuscript Division, Library of Congress, Journals & Diaries Collection.

Bruce, Philip A. *The Virginia Plutarch.* Chapel Hill, N.C.: University of North Carolina Press, 1929.

Bruce, Philip A. *Institutional History of Virginia in the 17th Century.* New York: Putnam's Sons, 1910.

Bryan, W. B. *A History of the National Capital.* New York: Macmillan, 1914.

Burnaby, Andrew. *Travels through the Middle Settlements in North America in the Years 1759 and 1760.* Ithaca, N.Y.: Cornell University Press, 1960.

Busey, Samuel Clagett. *Pictures of the City of Washington In the Past.* Washington: Ballantyne & Sons, 1898.

Calendar of Virginia State Papers: 1652 to 1869. Arranged, edited and printed under the authority and direction of H. W. Fourney, secretary of the Commonwealth and state librarian. Richmond, Virginia.

Callahan, Charles H. *Washington, the Man and the Mason.* Washington: Gibson Bros., 1933.

Carne, William F. *Alexandria Business Book.* Alexandria: M. Hill & Co., 1897.

Carne, William F. *The Charter and Laws of the City of Alexandria, Virginia, and An Historical Sketch of Its Government.* Alexandria: City Council, 1874.

Caton, James R. *Legislative Chronicles of the City of Alexandria.* Alexandria: Newell-Cole Co., Inc., 1933.

Chamberlain, Georgia S. "The Baptism of Pocahontas." *The Iron Worker,* (Summer, 1959).

Chapman, Sigismunda M. F. *A History of Chapman and Alexander Families.* Richmond: Dietz Printing Co., 1946.

Conway, Moncure Daniel. *Barons of the Potomac and Rappahannock.* New York: The Grolier Club, 1892.

Cutten, George Barton. *The Silversmiths of Virginia (Together with Watchmakers and Jewelers) from 1694 to 1850.* Richmond: Dietz Co., 1952.

Davis, Derring and others. *Alexandria Houses, 1750-1830.* New York: Architectural Book Publishing Co., Inc., 1946.

Davis, William A. *The Acts of Congress, In Relation to the District of Columbia from July 16, 1790, to March 4, 1831, inclusive and of the Legislatures of Virginia and Maryland.* Washington: Wm. A. Davis, 1831.

De Koven, Mrs. Reginald. *The Life and Letters of John Paul Jones.* New York: Chas. Scribner's Sons, 1913.

Diaries of George Washington. Edited by John Fitzpatrick. Boston: Houghton Mifflin Co., 1925.

Diary of John Adams. Cambridge: Harvard University Press, 1961.

Dorf, Philip. *Visualized American History.* New York: Oxford Book Co., 1934.

Elliot, Jonathan. *Historical Sketches of the Ten Miles Square, the Permanent Seat of the General Government of the United States.* Washington: Printed by Jonathan Elliot, Jr., 1830.

Executive Journals, Council of Colonial Virginia. (Transcript of extracts.) Richmond, n.d.

Ferri-Pisani, Camille. *Prince Napoleon In America, 1861.* Bloomington, Ind.: Indiana University Press, 1959.

Fiske, John. *Old Virginia and Her Neighbors.* Boston: Houghton Mifflin, 1897.

Fithian, Philip Vickers. *Journal & Letters of Philip Vickers Fithian, 1773-1774.* Williamsburg: Colonial Williamsburg, Inc., 1943.

Ford, Worthington Chauncey. *The Writings of George Washington.* New York: Putnam's, 1889-1893.

Freeman, Douglas Southall. *George Washington: A Biography.* New York: Chas. Scribner's Sons, 1948.

Freeman, Douglas Southall. *Robert E. Lee: A Biography.* New York: Chas. Scribner's Sons, 1935.

Gahn, Bessie Wilmarth. *Original Patentees of Land at Washington Prior to 1700.* Silver Spring, Md.: Printed by Westland, 1936.

General Washington's Last Guard of Honor. Alexandria: Mount Vernon Chapter, Daughters of the American Revolution, 1957.

"George Mason: The Forgotten Statesman 1725-1792." Mexico City *Daily Bulletin,* July 4, 1961.

George Washington Atlas. Editor, Lawrence Martin. Washington: United States George Washington Bicentennial Commission, 1932.

"George Washington Bicentennial News." Alexandria: *Alexandria Gazette,* October 1930 to December 1931.

Gibson, Sister Laurita. "Catholic Women of Colonial Maryland." Unpublished Master's thesis, Catholic University of America, 1939.

Grant, Dorothy F. *Adventurous Lady: Margaret Brent of Maryland.* New York: Kenedy Publishing Co., 1957.

Hallowell, Benjamin. *Autobiography of Benjamin Hallowell.* Philadelphia: Friends' Book Assoc., 1883.

Harrison, Fairfax. *Landmarks of Old Prince William.* Richmond: Old Dominion Press, 1924.

Harrison, Fairfax, *Proprietors of the Northern Neck.* Richmond: Old Dominion Press, 1926.

Harrison, Fairfax. *Virginia Land Grants.* Richmond: Old Dominion Press, 1925.

Hayden, Horace Edwin. *Virginia Genealogies.* Washington: Rare Book Shop, 1931.

Hening, William Waller. *The Statutes At Large: Being a Collection of All the Laws of Virginia from the First Session of the Legislature in the Year 1619.* New York: R. & W. & G. Bartow, 1823.

Herndon, Melvin. *Tobacco In Colonial Virginia.* Williamsburg: Virginia 350th Anniversary Celebration, 1957.

Historical Sketch of Ann Pamela Cunningham. New York: Marion Press, 1929. (Mount Vernon Ladies' Association.)

Historical Society of Fairfax County: Yearbook. Fairfax, Virginia.

History of An Expedition Against Fort DuQuesne, in 1755; under Major-General Edward Braddock. Edited from the original manuscript by Winthrop Sargent. Philadelphia: Lippincott, Grambo & Co., 1855.

"History of the Boundaries of Arlington County, Virginia." Arlington: Office of the County Manager, 1957.

History of the Theological Seminary in Virginia. Edited by Rev. A. R. Goodwin. Rochester, N.Y.: DuBois Press, 1924.

Howe, Henry. *Historical Collections of Virginia.* Charleston, S.C.: Babcock & Co., 1846.

Jackson, Eugene B. *Romance of Historic Alexandria: A Guide to the Old City.* Atlanta, Ga.: A. B. Caldwell Publishing Co., 1921.

Janson, Charles Wm. *The Stranger In America, 1793 to 1806.* New York: Press of the Pioneers, Inc., 1935.

Jeffersonian Cyclopedia. Edited by John P. Foley. New York & London: Funk & Wagnalls Co., 1900.

Johnson, Gerald W. *Mount Vernon: The Story of a Shrine.* New York: Random House, 1953.

Jones, Hugh. *Present State of Virginia.* New York: Joseph Sabin, 1865.

"Jones Point Lighthouse." Unpublished Records of the Mount Vernon Chapter, Daughters of the American Revolution, 1953.

Journal of Nicholas Cresswell: 1774-1777. New York: Dial Press, 1924.

Journals of the Continental Congress. Washington, Government Printing Office, 1904.

Journals of the House of Burgesses of Virginia. Edited by John Pendleton Kennedy. Richmond: 1905.

Kabler, Dorothy H. *A History of Burke & Herbert's Century of Service to Alexandria and Virginia 1852-1952.* Alexandria: Newell-Cole Co., 1952.

Kabler, Dorothy H. *Port on the Potomac.* Alexandria: Newell-Cole Co., 1949.

Kabler, Dorothy H. *The Story of Gadsby's Tavern.* Alexandria: Newell-Cole Co., 1952.

Kent, James. Personal Papers, 1793-1794. Manuscript Division, Library of Congress.

Land Patent Books, 1652-1679. Land Office, Richmond, Virginia.

Land Records of Long Standing, 1742-1770. Fairfax County Courthouse, Fairfax, Va.

Leech, Margaret. *Reveille In Washington.* New York: Harper Bros., 1941.

"Letter from Tobias Lear to Thomas Jefferson." American Historical Review. (v.28) New York: Macmillan Co.

Lindsey, Mary. *Historic Homes and Landmarks of Alexandria, Virginia.* Alexandria: Newell-Cole Co., 1931, 1947.

Long, Florence. "Historical Sketch of Alexandria's Oldest Daily Newspaper." Alexandria: Gazette Printing Office, 1938.

Lonn, Ella. *Foreigners In the Confederacy.* Chapel Hill, N.C.: University of North Carolina Press, 1940.

Lossing, Benson. *Pictorial Field Book of the American Republic.* New York: Virtue & Yorston, 1870.

Lowdermilk, W. H. *History of Cumberland, Maryland.* Washington: 1878.

Madison, James. *The Writings of James Madison.* New York: G. P. Putnam's Sons, 1900-1910.

Mann, Harrison. "Retrocession." *Arlington Historical Magazine.* Arlington Historical Society, Nos. 1 & 2, 1957 & 1958.

Marine Railway & Coal Co., Inc. vs. U.S.A. Re: Battery Cove, Alexandria, No. 3312 In the Court of Appeals, D.C., Oct. Term, 1919, v.2.

Maryland Gazette.

Mason, John. Reminiscences, letters, etc. Philip Dawson Papers, privately owned. Unpublished. (Includes letters by George Mason.)

Mathews, Catherine V. *Andrew Ellicott, His Life and Letters.* New York: Grafton Press, 1908.

McCardell, Lee. *Ill-Starred General: Braddock of the Coldstream Guards.* Pittsburgh: University of Pittsburgh Press, 1958.

McGroarty, William Buckner. *The Old Presbyterian Meeting House at Alexandria, Virginia.* Richmond: Wm. Byrd Press, 1940.

McGuire, Judith Brockenbrough. *Diary of a Southern Refugee, During the War.* New York: E. J. Hale & Son, 1867.

Meade, William. *Old Churches, Ministers and Families of Virginia.* Philadelphia: J. B. Lippincott Co., 1854.

Miller, Helen Hill. *George Mason, Constitutionalist.* Cambridge: Harvard University Press, 1938.

Miller, Helen Hill. *George Mason of Gunston Hall.* Lorton, Va.: The Board of Regents of Gunston Hall, 1958.

Moore, Gay Montague. *Seaport in Virginia: George Washington's Alexandria.* Richmond: Garrett & Massie, Inc., 1949.

Morison, Samuel Eliot. *John Paul Jones: A Sailor's Biography.* Boston: Little, Brown & Co., 1959.

Morrison, William A. *Stranger's Guide to the City of Washington and Its Vicinity.* Washington City: Wm. M. Morrison, 1842.

Mount Vernon Guards. "Constitution, By Laws and Minutes: July 4, 1842 to Sept. 11, 1853." Unpublished: Alexandria Library.

Mount Vernon Ladies' Association of the Union. Mount Vernon: Annual Reports.

Muir, Dorothy Troth. *Potomac Interlude.* Washington: Mount Vernon Print Shop, 1943.

Muir, Dorothy Troth. *Presence of A Lady.* Washington: Mount Vernon Publishing Co., 1946.

Mysteries of Washington City During Several Months of the Session of the 28th Congress. By A Citizen of Ohio. Washington: G. A. Sage, 1844.

National Intelligencer. Washington, D.C.

Nugent, Nell Marion. *Cavaliers and Pioneers.* Richmond: Dietz Press, 1934.

Our Town: 1749-1865. Alexandria Association. Richmond: Dietz Printing Co., 1956.

Perry, B. F. *Reminiscences of Mrs. Louisa Cunningham.* Privately printed: South Carolina, 1874.

Powell, Mary G. *The History of Old Alexandria, Virginia: From July 13, 1749 to May 24, 1861.* Richmond: Wm. Byrd Press, 1928.

(Index to above: prepared by the Alexandria Library, 1962.)

Proceedings of the Board of Trustees, Town of Alexandria, Virginia: 1749-1767. Unpublished: Office of the City Manager, Alexandria.

Randall, Ruth Painter. *Colonel Elmer Ellsworth.* Boston: Little, Brown & Co., 1960.

Records of the Columbia Historical Society. Washington: Published by the Society, 1895-1961.

Report on the Potential for Waterborne Commerce on the Potomac River at Alexandria, Virginia and Washington, D.C. Prepared by the Virginia State Ports Authority, Norfolk, Va., 1957.

Robertson, J. Dallas. "The Civil War Chapter In the History of Alexandria, Virginia." (Thesis, Randolph-Macon College, 1949.)

Robinson, W. Stitt, Jr. *Mother Earth, Land Grants in Virginia, 1606-1699.* Edited by Earl Grett Swem. Williamsburg: Virginia 350th Anniversary Celebration Corp., 1957.

Roscoe, Theodore and Fred Freeman. *Picture History of the United States Navy, from Old Navy to New, 1776-1897.* New York: Scribner's, 1956.

Rose, C. B., Jr. "A Glimpse of Arlington in the 18th Century." *Arlington Historical Magazine,* No. 2, 1958.

Rose, C. B., Jr. *The Indians of Arlington.* Office of the County Manager, Arlington, Virginia, 1957.

Rothery, Agnes. *New Roads in Old Virginia.* Boston: Houghton, Mifflin Co., 1929.

Rothgeb, Roy M. "An Analysis of the Rise, Decline and Possibilities for Redevelopment of the Port of Alexandria." (Master's Thesis, 1957; copy in Alexandria Library.)

Rowland, Kate Mason. *The Life of George Mason: 1725-1792.* New York: G. P. Putnam's Sons, 1892.

Royall, Ann. *Sketches of History, Life and Manners in the United States.* New Haven: Printed for the author, 1826.

Schoepf, Johann David. *Travels in the Confederation: 1783-1784.* Philadelphia: Wm. J. Campbell, 1911.

Schondau, Frederick F. *Freemasonry's Great Monument.* Washington: Masonic Service Assoc., 1957 (2nd ed.).

Scott, Richard Marshall, Sr., and Richard Marshall Scott, Jr. *Diaries.* (From 1811 to 1825, and 1846 to 1855.) Unpublished: owned by Bruce C. Gunnell.

Shepherd, Samuel. *Statutes At Large of Virginia, from October Session 1792 to December Session 1806, inclusive.* Richmond: Printed by Samuel Shepherd, 1835.

Slaughter, Philip. *The History of Truro Parish, In Virginia.* Edited by Edward L. Goodwin. Philadelphia: Geo. W. Jacobs & Co., 1907.

Smith, Margaret Bayard. *The First Forty Years of Washington Society.* New York: Scribner's Sons, 1906.

Smoot, Betty Carter. *Days in An Old Town.* Washington: Judd & Detweiler, Inc., 1934.

Snowden, W. H. *Some Old Historic Landmarks of Virginia and Maryland Described In A Handbook for the Tourist Over the Washington-Virginia Railway.* Privately published by William H. Snowden, 1904, (7th ed.).

"Souvenir Program: 100th Anniversary, Richmond, Fredericksburg & Potomac Railroad Company." Published by the Company, 1934.

Stanard, Mary Newton. *Colonial Virginia: Its People and Customs.* Philadelphia: J. B. Lippincott Co., 1917.

Stephens, Edward L. *One Hundred and Fifty Years for Christ: 1795-1945.* Alexandria: Privately published, 1945.

Stetson, Charles W. *Four Mile Run Land Grants*. Washington, Mimeoform Press, 1935.

Stetson, Charles W. *Washington and His Neighbors*. Richmond: Garrett & Massie, 1956.

Sunday Star. The Washington Star, Washington, D.C.: April 8, 1906.

Thomas Jefferson Papers. Edited by Julian P. Boyd. Princeton: Princeton University Press, 1950.

Tindall, William. *Standard History of the City of Washington*. Knoxville, Tenn.: H. W. Crew & Co., 1914.

Torbert, Alice Coyle. *Eleanor Calvert and Her Circle*. New York: Wm. Frederick Press, 1950.

Ties. Southern Railway Systems Magazine. Washington: Feb. 1951; Dec. 1958.

Townsend, George A. *Rustics In Rebellion: A Yankee Reporter on the Way to Richmond, 1861-1865*. Chapel Hill, N.C.: University of North Carolina Press, 1950.

Tyler's Historical & Genealogical Quarterly. Richmond: Whittet & Shepperson, 1920.

United States Census Bureau Publication. Government Printing Office. 1960.

Virginia: A Guide to the Old Dominion. American Guide Series. New York: Oxford University Press, 1956 edition.

Virginia Gazette. Williamsburg, Va.: August 25, 1774.

Virginia Magazine of History & Biography. Published quarterly by the Virginia Historical Society. Richmond: printed by Whittet & Shepperson.

Virginia 350 Anniversary Collection. Williamsburg: Colonial Williamsburg, Inc., 1957.

Wall, Charles C. *Notes on the Early History of Mount Vernon*. Reprinted from the William & Mary Quarterly, 3rd serv., v. 2, April 1945.

Warden, David Baillie. *A Chorographical and Statistical Description of the District of Columbia*. Paris: 1816. (Printed and sold by Smith.)

Warfield, Edgar. *A Confederate Soldier's Memoirs*. Richmond: Masonic Home Press, Inc., 1936.

War of the Rebellion. Official Records. Washington: Government Printing Office, 1901.

Waterman, Thomas T. *Mansions of Virginia*. Chapel Hill, N.C.: University of North Carolina Press, 1946.

Wedderburn, Alexander J. *Historic Alexandria, Virginia*. Privately printed, 1899 and 1907.

Wertenbaker, Thomas J. *The Planters of Colonial Virginia*. Princeton: Princeton University Press, 1922.

Wharton, Anne H. *Social Life In the Early Republic.* Philadelphia: Lippincott, 1902.

Wharton, James. *The Bounty of the Chesapeake: Fishing In Colonial Virginia.* Williamsburg: Virginia 350 Anniversary Celebration, 1957.

Whittington Diary. (From May 24, 1861 to the end of the Civil War.) Unpublished. Alexandria Library.

Wilkes, Marion R. *Rosemont and Its Famous Daughter.* Washington: Privately published, 1947.

William and Mary College Quarterly Historical Magazine. Published by the College. Richmond: printed by Whittet & Shepperson.

William Ramsay's Ledger. June 9, 1753 to June 21, 1757. Unpublished. Smithsonian Institution, Washington, D.C.

Wilstach, Paul. *Potomac Landings.* Indianapolis: Bobbs-Merrill Co., 1932.

Wise, George. *A History of the Seventeenth Virginia Regiment C. S. A.* Baltimore: Kelly, Piet & Co., 1870.

Writings of Thomas Jefferson. Edited by Albert Ellery Bergh. Washington: Thomas Jefferson Memorial Association of the United States, 1907.

Yearbook of the Alexandria Association. Published by the Association. Alexandria: printed by Newell-Cole Co., 1957.

Index

251

253